T3-BNG-801

MGEN
MR943

Public Library Services to Business

Rosemarie Riechel

BIBLIOTHÈQUES
uOttawa
LIBRARIES

Neal-Schuman Publishers, Inc.
New York   **London**

630485/98

Published by Neal-Schuman Publishers, Inc.
100 Varick Street
New York, NY 10013

Copyright © 1994 by Rosemarie Riechel

All rights reserved. Reproduction of this book, in whole or in
part, without written permission of the publisher is prohibited.

Printed and bound in the United States of America

Library of Congress Cataloging-in-Publication Data

Riechel , Rosemarie , 1937 -
    Public library services to business / Rosemarie Riechel .
       p.   cm.
    Includes bibliographical references (p .) and index.
    ISBN 1-55570-168-X :
      1. Public libraries -- United States -- Services to business and
industry.   I. Title .
    Z675.B8R54   1994
      027.6 ' 9 -- dc20   94 - 7018
                                            CIP

Z
675
.B8
R54
1994

Acknowledgments

This book was inspired by hundreds of businesspeople, whose information needs and frustrations became mine during my years as a public library information professional.

I wish to express my gratitude to the many public, corporate, academic and state librarians, as well as the Special Libraries Association chapter presidents, who took the time to complete the survey questionnaire. Without their cooperation and commitment to business information and reference service, this book could not have been completed.

Grateful acknowledgment is made to Virginia H. Mathews, my editor, for her encouragement in the creation of this book, and her skillful guidance in its development and refinement.

I also wish to acknowledge Janice W. Bain, past president of the Florida chapter of the Special Libraries Association and Head of Access Services at the University of Florida, and Nancy M. Bolt, of the Colorado Department of Education, State Library and Adult Education Office, for the invaluable information they have supplied.

I owe a special debt of gratitude to Maxine Bleiweis, Director of the Lucy Robbins Welles Library, Dr. Carrie Coolbaugh, Assistant Director of the Commerce Public Library, Angela Baughman Bowie, of the Cleveland Research Center, Cleveland Public Library, and Kay Cunningham of the Science/Business/Social Science Department, Memphis/Shelby County Public Library and Information Center.

Thanks are due also to Billy Kenny, Assistant Manager, Public Relations, New York Public Library, Mary M. Grant, Director of the Center for Business Research, Long Island University, C.W. Post Campus, and Dr. Shawkey Karas, Professor, Southern Connecticut State University.

Finally, special acknowledgment is made to my family for their steadfast support.

Contents

Foreword

Corporations and businesses of all sizes pay property tax in the communities in which they are located. If for no other reason, this tax support should give them at least minimal expectations that local public libraries will include materials and services geared to their needs. Beyond the tax incentive, why should public libraries be concerned about developing working relationships with the corporations and businesses in their town or city?

The most frequent, immediate response is that businesses can be called on to supply monetary and in-kind resources when a library needs them. Although this may have been true in the past, businesses are being hit from all sides by increasing numbers of good causes that need support. If the public library has established a reputation for serving business needs, that support will be more readily forthcoming.

Strong local health is a positive benefit for public libraries that rely on taxes for funding. The public library can make a significant contribution to local economic development. Small businesses have few places other than the public library to turn to for information on how to manage a business in a profitable way. Profitable small businesses enhance the economic stability of any region. Public libraries in many areas perform information gathering services for local government agencies, aiding in bringing new businesses into the area, among other things.

In Arizona, the Department of Library Archives & Public Records formed an economic development committee comprised of librarians and representatives of business and economic development organizations from around the state. A core bibliography of materials for libraries to use in working with local business and economic development agencies was created. The state library has purchased sets of these materials, and more than 28 Economic Development Information

Centers (EDICs) have opened around the state. Working with the Small Business Development Centers (SBDCs) of the U.S. Small Business Administration, and local economic development council, the EDICs provide information resources and services, counseling, and seminars on topics of interest to the local business communities.

A Library Partners program in Illinois, pairs public libraries and local chambers of commerce to work together to meet each other's needs. Each participating community submits an annual report outlining their cooperative activities. An annual awards program recognizes outstanding efforts. In the Schaumberg Public Library, one of the pilot sites for the library Partners program, the entire reference staff has been trained to respond to business-related inquiries. Of approximately 41,000 information requests annually, more than half are from businesses.

There is a demonstarted need for public library service to business, not only in Schaumberg, Illinois, but anywhere in the country where it has been established, publicized, and built on a recognition of the needs of all parties in partnership.

Having worked in both public and corporate libraries, I can attest to the many benefits on both sides from cooperative arrangements. For example, corporate libraries frequently need generalist materials and information, but it doesn't always make economic sense for them to stock them in their collections. The local public library is the logical place for corporate librarians to turn to augment their in-house collection. Conversely, when the local public library is looking for business expertise, equipment or materials, or contributions, the corporate librarian who has used and benefited from the public library's services is the perfect entry point into the resources of corporations.

The opportunities for cooperative relationships between public libraries and local businesses are limited only by the creative thinking and immigration of those involved. Rosemarie Riechel has provided an overview of some of the areas in which libraries and businesses have cooperated. Her book creates a frame work for exploring the needs to be met and opportunities to be recognized when attention is directed to this sometimes neglected segment of public library service.

Susan S. DiMattia

Susan S. DiMattia is a Business Information Consultant based in Stamford, CT. She is the editor of Library Hotline and Corporate Library Update, and a former bank librarian and business specialist for public libraries.

Introduction

The purpose of this book is to examine present trends in public library service to the business community and the current level of cooperation between public and corporate libraries, in order to define in detail the components necessary to the development, maintenance, and expansion of service to this special user group.

Public library service to the business community has long been encouraged by library leaders. Such service is likely to result in an appreciation of the significance of public libraries, along with some valuable support for public funding. Experience has shown that in some cases public library-supplied information helped people to better run their businesses. In contrast, corporate libraries must prove their value as active contributors to the profit-making function of the companies they were established to serve. The task of justifying the value of libraries as indispensable sources of information necessary for the economic success of business and industry, employers and employees, and the community as a whole, requires considerable skill and energy. It is not easy to show a correlation between library use and "bottom-line" profit.

Librarians have long recognized that libraries have an economic mission beyond that of recreation or education, but efforts to define it, develop it, and promote it have evolved slowly. It takes time to stimulate a appreciation of books and non-book resources as primary tools for the development and enrichment of lives and livelihoods. The task is twofold:

1. To respond to the present and anticipated needs of the population served—that of a community or company;
2. To actively encourage the use of libraries as institutions that promote social values, education, cultural, philosophical, scien-

tific, technical, and vocational knowledge and understanding. (At the present time job and career flexibility for patrons is high on the agenda for most libraries.)

The rapid and constant expansion of business and industry, along with the emergence of the working class, highlighted the potential value of public libraries to a growing special user group. The opportunity to help fulfill the economic goals of companies, and to foster the self-education and intellectual stimulation of employees was used creatively to form a cooperative link between public libraries and businesses.

In the nineteenth century this cooperation originated with the establishment of mercantile and mechanics' libraries in large cities at a time when much attention was given to social and moral values, and the promotion of "proper" cultural and recreational activities and education. For a fee, young workers, apprentices, merchants' clerks, as well as any other member of the community, including women, could gain access to a collection of popular literature, enjoy educational programs, and engage in a variety of morally uplifting and socially correct activities, such as discussion groups, concerts, and museum exhibits. Mechanics' libraries were controlled by employers with a paternalistic attitude, heavily weighted with self-interest, toward the young fellows coming to the big city to learn a trade. In exchange for the required dues, these workers would be protected from the sins of society and encouraged to focus attention on the job. To stay alive, mercantile and mechanics' libraries had to attract and retain members by meeting the constant demand for new material and programs. The expense of this, along with a lack of clearly defined goals, led to their demise or merger with newly established public libraries. Even though these libraries had direct ties to business, there is little evidence to show that they were used to provide information for economic benefit.

In the 1830s, factory and club libraries were established and subsidized by employers with a concern for the moral and intellectual development, and educational and recreational needs of the unskilled factory and mill laborers in their employ. However, these subscription libraries were not accessible during business hours.

Enlightened managers encouraged employee-operated club libraries. Some, the Steel Works Club, for example, went beyond the traditional book collection, offering such recreational facilities as bowling alleys, a billiard room, and baths. Its library was unique as well. In 1903, along with the usual popular titles, it included some technical books and industry-related periodicals—a hint of the future emergence of the corporate library. Factory and club libraries were fazed out as new cooperative links were developed between free public libraries and businesses.

Some successful business leaders were inspired to donate money to build free public libraries in an effort to encourage the self-education and recreational habits of not only the employees, but of the entire population of the communities in which they lived. The most noted of these philanthropists is Andrew Carnegie (1835-1919), who initially used some of his iron and steel fortune to support factory libraries. In time his money was used for the development of the free public library, with collections that included traditional and popular works as well as material covering a wide variety of subjects that would encourage vocational improvement.

The public libraries in the commercial or industrial areas in cities were most closely associated with businesses. These libraries conducted outreach programs aimed at bringing services to people in factories, banks, large stores, offices, social centers, and more. Library service was extended in two new ways:

1 . The delivery station which had no collection, but was equipped with a catalog or a list of titles that one could scan, note the choices, and accept delivery at a later date;
2. The deposit station, which consisted of a rotating collection that travelled from one station to another over a defined period of time.

The deposit station was the more successful of the two programs, probably because the users could examine the books themselves. They were simple to operate and effectively extended public library service beyond the main library and its limited number of branches. The general collection located in a particular firm was frequently augmented with sources that met some technical and vocational information needs—evidence that company libraries began with informal collections of materials.

The popularity of the deposit library faded early in the twentieth century because it could not support the ever-increasing publication of business and technical materials. A deepening interest in emerging business administration and management theories, and new technology related to commercial enterprise, meant that the time had come to demonstrate the importance of public libraries even more effectively by developing special business/technical collections that would target local business and industrial needs with greater depth.

John Cotton Dana (1856-1929) of the Newark Public Library actively courted businessmen to persuade them to use public library collections for their own benefit, and ultimately for the success of their businesses. Dana's promotional methods were successful and are similar to those used today:

- Distribution of a list of business sources available;
- Circular mailings advertising the special business resources available;
- Surveying and analyzing the use of library collections by businesses;
- Preparing special bibliographies on business-related subjects.

Dana's vigorous courtship of local businesses was rewarded with the establishment of a special business branch in the downtown commercial/financial district of the city in 1904. Its modest collection of general works and city directories rapidly expanded to include business periodicals, government documents, books on commerce, banking, manufacturing, law, insurance, real estate, retail business, and more.

This method of pursuit and capture of the interest and support of the business community gradually spread to other urban areas. Separate business branches, business departments in central libraries, or combined business/technology collections began to appear in a number of major cities: Portland, Oregon, Minneapolis, Minnesota, Rochester, New York, Omaha, Nebraska and Brooklyn, New York, to name but a few.

At the same time Dana was also engaged in the task of calling attention to the growing number of private business libraries—among the earliest ones were those serving insurance, chemical, pharmaceutical, and engineering companies. Disparate collections had to be consolidated to increase service efficiency. Therefore the members of the Special Libraries Association, founded in 1909, had to define the purpose and significance of their group of libraries, to identify methods of justifying continued growth, development, and funding.[1] Dana's twofold interest and dedication to public and corporate libraries greatly influenced the development of modern business collections that meet the needs of the communities they serve.

Successive surveys of company personnel indicate that the benefits their libraries provide are generally unclear to them. Public library use studies consistently show that many queries received are business-related; however, service to this constituency is too often unfocused. If the business community does not use the available special services and resources of public and corporate libraries, they cannot gain an appreciation of the value that access to a wide variety of relevant data could have to economic growth and well-being.

The technique of proclaiming library service as accessible to all, regardless of the location of the collection, proved to be a powerful method of attracting new users. The simplest request for a word definition or chemical formula, or a more time-consuming task (for example, compiling demographics for market research, gathering current data on a particular company, industry or product, or locating patent records for an inventor might be easily satisfied without the businesspeople spending much personal time or effort—and without the requisite trip to the library. The telephone was the perfect instrument. Not too long after Bell introduced his invention in 1876, it became an essential piece of equipment in offices, factories and stores. Rapid communication from business to business, from business to customer, and from business to company library became possible.

In the 1930s, public library telephone reference was advertised as a service of great practical value to businessmen. The popularity of reference service by telephone grew with the increasing demand for quick information. But the early collections were small and general—usually including an almanac, a census and statistical abstract of the United States, a postal guide, a secretary's handbook, a newspaper and periodicals directory, some telephone books, and a book of etiquette.

Telephone reference service grew along with the demand for information. By the 1950s many urban libraries had added this special service, and had begun to examine its organization and collection in an effort to streamline access and improve the quality of the reference and information retrieval process. Some libraries, such as the Brooklyn, Minneapolis, and St. Louis public libraries developed separate telephone reference services. Many of the queries received were related to business or technology, but librarians also dealt with a good number of requests for information in a wide variety of other subject areas.[2] For reasons of call-overload, insufficient staff, or the desire to concentrate solely on requests from the business community, telephone reference quickly became a special service of public library business libraries or departments.

The 1950s and 1960s marked a period of rapid economic growth. As a result, communities changed and expanded. The downtown business districts of large cities continued to house corporate offices, banks, stock and trade markets, and legal and governmental offices, many of them establishing libraries to provide information and special services for executives and employees. But smaller areas of retail trade, small- and medium-size businesses, suburban shopping malls, commercial parks, factories, and wholesale/retail outlets appeared outside the traditional geographic center of private and public enterprise. As businesses scattered throughout the areas they served, public libraries had to explore different methods of providing direct service to those in different locations, while retaining their focus on the centralized business collection. Clearly, the standard patron referral to the main library or special business branch, without consideration of user convenience, was no longer acceptable as a regular practice. So the development of adequate collections suited to local business information needs became essential—as did finding a solution to the problem of funding them, particularly in small- or medium-size libraries or branches.

Business information needs have been influenced by economic and social problems, especially from the 1970's to the present. A slow economy, inflation, high unemployment, the balance of trade, the global marketplace, less consumer credit and spending, environmental concerns, urban blight, government cutbacks, and more resulted in a pressing need for up-to-date information essential to all aspects of living. Today, more than ever before, successful community life is based on knowledge. Although corporate libraries have to develop and deliver effective, customized services to a specific user group, public libraries are obliged to quickly and accurately provide all the information needed to a diverse business clientele, including:

• Personnel from public and private enterprise;
• Large corporations with or without their own special libraries;
• The general public interested in insurance, investments, interest rates, financing, stock quotes, real estate, and more;
• The job seeker in need of material on resume writing, occupational outlook, new vocations, and individual company histories, background, and financial data;
• The entrepreneur in need of books, periodicals and other print and non-print resources on markets, small business management, making money, advertising, and more;
• Rural area craftsmen, traders, farmers, animal breeders, small business owners, writers, and inventors with a variety of business and technical information needs;
• Graduate and undergraduate students of business and industry.

This expanded business community must have full access to the entire universe of print and non-print data via a cooperative information and communication network consisting of all types of libraries—public, corporate, academic, and association. The virtual explosion of business information makes the efficient use of technology essential if this network is to successfully retrieve and deliver information with the speed that is required in the competitive business world of the 1990s and the twenty-first century.

Computers are now as commonplace as telephones in business offices, banks, factories, retail stores, and in most libraries. They allow for the creation of a strong link between public libraries and the business community, as well as between the corporate library and the public library. Computer-based reference and research service is a necessity in this era of rapid proliferation of online search systems and databases. The number of business-oriented databases available in online or CD-ROM formats is remarkable; some of them do not have printed counterparts because the data contained in them becomes outdated so rapidly it would not be cost-effective to publish them in hard copy. It is imperative that company libraries offer access to online databases because the quality and timeliness of information is a prerequisite to corporate success. But businesses without their own libraries, or which lack all or some of the vendor systems available, should be able to turn to the local public library. If public libraries cannot provide the entire business community with automated information retrieval, via a free or fee-based service, they will be viewed as static institutions, with collections only as current as the publication dates of hard copy sources. Potential clients will certainly go elsewhere for their information—to academic libraries, information brokers, and perhaps other corporate libraries or related associations.

In addition to commercial databases, in-house online or CD-ROM databases, such as a local business directory, might be made available for library reference use or as a print or on-disk source for purchase. Their value would be increased if they were also accessible system-wide, regionally, or statewide via a cooperative communication network. On a larger scale, a statewide network might provide a gateway to legislative, job, career, or demographic databases, for example, as an effective means of information sharing for member libraries of all types.

The marriage of computer technology and cooperative cataloging has effectively linked libraries to speed up the interlibrary loan process. A library's catalog might be searched in all branches of a system, as well as in other libraries, company offices, and in the homes of clients who own a computer and modem. On a larger scale, cooperative regional, state, multistate, and national networks allow online access to the collections of member libraries. Electronic mail speeds up the interlibrary loan process even further, after searching the bibliographic database, requests for particular items can be sent directly to the library, along with a request for overnight delivery.

Telefascimile is not new to business because the cost-effectiveness of rapid inter-office and intra-company communications was quickly recognized. In the 1980s fax service was used as a powerful tool in quite a number of public libraries, from large urban systems to small suburban and rural libraries with inadequate information resources. This technology made it possible to photocopy information from books, newspapers, and journals available in hard copy, on microfilm, or microfiche, and deliver it within minutes to other libraries, business offices, or residences. New telefascimile applications, using a touchtone telephone, make it possible to access a database, follow a voice menu to guide one through the information selection steps, and have the requested data delivered directly to the caller's fax machine. Speeding up document delivery in this way certainly has some exciting possibilities for businesses, corporate and public libraries.[3]

Just how do public libraries meet the information demands of a current and potential business clientele, enhance the hard copy collection, and fully embrace technology to be able to offer the ultimate in service? When faced with inflation, increased staffing/materials/equipment costs, reduced government funding, a decline in corporate giving, and a lack of enthusiasm for adequate tax support on the part of a financially burdened community, administrators and reference librarians must identify barriers to quality service, examine and revise policies, and actively court the business community.

Library use studies consistently find that businesspeople generally are not aware of public libraries and their collections. Since they tend to rely on their fellow employees, friends, trade associations, salespersons, or journals they see in the office or personally subscribe to, a vigorous campaign for local library use by businesspersons must be pursued. Similarly, corporate librarians must prove that the use of their libraries, and/or cooperative links with other libraries for either primary or supplementary services, is vital to employee and company success. Clearly, an institution of unknown value would not be actively supported.

Librarians have sometimes feared that publicity might cause a flood of queries that cannot be managed by the existing staff. On the other hand, advertising such attractive services as cooperative networks, telephone reference, rapid information delivery, online information retrieval, customized reference and research, increases awareness of a library's value and may lead to more adequate funding.

Public libraries are understaffed, underfunded, and reluctant to commit time and energy to continuing a study of the community. This is essential to develop a profile of the business population, focus on its specific perceptions of the library, determine its information needs and select materials that will support these needs.

A staff/funding shortage is also the reason many public libraries do not embrace computer technology with total enthusiasm. As with expensive hard copy sources, automated information retrieval systems are perceived as too costly. Also, the time needed to find alternative funding to support the enhancement of business resources and services is thought to detract from other library activities. The staff, as well as an unenlightened administration, too often believe that there are so many new business-related online and CD-ROM databases available that it is not possible to keep up with the field, satisfy all patrons, devote time to training staff to use computers and automated systems, teach patrons how to use hard copy and automated resources, and conduct searches for clients.

Following the tradition of free and open access, many public librarians insist that online database searching should be available at no cost to the client. Then, in the name of budget structures, various "free" limitations are placed on searching—number of citations, abstracts, or full text records printed, time spent per search, and number of searches per patron are common. The idea of exhausting all manual sources first is popular, but impractical for users who need information immediately. Many public librarians stick to their ethical and professional convictions on the subject of fee-based service, insisting that a tax-supported public library must be open to all to be served equally. Without automated information retrieval systems, public library users will be served equally poorly.

Clearly, barriers to full library service to the business community must be identified and eliminated. Free and open access to resources in all formats should be guaranteed by continuous evaluation of reference service, staff expertise and community needs, along with active promotion of library service and cooperative efforts.

NOTES

1. A concise historical overview appears in Kruzas, Anthony Thomas. *Business and Industrial Libraries in the United States, 1820-1940.* New York: Special Libraries Association, 1965.

2. For more detailed background information see Riechel, Rosemarie. *Improving Telephone Information and Reference Service in Public Libraries.* Hamden, CT: Library Professional Publications, 1987.

3. Lachman, Christine E. "Fax-On-Demand: An Introduction." *Library Hi Tech* 9 (1991): 7-24.

1

Service Barriers

Do you know that the public library provides business information and reference service?

Does the staff take an interest in all of your information needs?

Does the information presented to you answer your questions?

Is the data retrieved for you delivered in a timely manner?

Do you trust the public library as a reliable and efficient source of information?

If the majority of the members of the business community can answer these questions in the affirmative, their responses indicate that a successful relationship with the public library has been created for business and industry in the area served. If librarians ask these questions of the business population, they are well on their way to collecting the evidence they need to determine whether or not they function as the primary source of information for this special group.

On the whole, the quality of reference service to business is deficient, primarily because self-examination and/or continued analysis of a variety of evaluative data is often not considered vital. The usual reason for this is staff and budget constraints. Qualitative and quantitative analysis of patron attitudes, use of resources and services, staff attitudes, success rates, collection development practices, information retrieval and delivery processes, the patron's perception of the library's mission, and the role of the staff is needed to define what service to the business community should be. The common practice is to assume that resources, services and policies are on target, and that the available resources and services are effectively, efficiently, and adequately fulfilling information needs. As a result of conclusions based on such assumptions, many public libraries do not capture the attention of a potentially large business-related clientele. Indeed, in some cases, corporate librarians hesitate to make referrals. Plodding interlibrary loan service and limited or no access to online databases does not foster the good will of large corporations, the biggest tax payers and supporters of the public library budget. Also, library professionals should not assume that companies that lack or lose their libraries, small businesses, entrepreneurs, the unemployed, researchers, technicians, and others in need of information related to business and industry, are adequately served without appropriate analysis of the make-up of the business community and its diverse information needs.

Businesspersons are disadvantaged if the library's resources and services are unknown to them. A vigorous and on-going marketing campaign is the best way to spread the word. But many libraries tend not to market library service actively to the business community. The following reasons for not promoting library service to the business community, all of which were reflected in a significant portion of the surveys, reinforce the author's research and many years of experience in the field:

- Insufficient budget and staff time to go out into the community to listen to the needs of clients and potential users, gain their trust and cooperation, involve them in decisions regarding programs, services and resources;
- A lack of appreciation of the importance of marketing library service to the business community—the quality service-library support connection;
- Failure to appreciate the importance of the library's role as information provider for the economic good of business, the library itself, and the community;
- Lack of motivation and clear vision on the part of the professionals and the administrators;
- A narrow view of the significance of ever-changing information technology to business clientele;
- An attitude of complacency;
- A lack of energy for surveys, focus groups, breakfasts, conventions, exhibits, the development of workshops,training programs, coupled with the fear of neglecting other library services;
- Insufficient staff for community involvement programs;
- A lack of interest/knowledge in subjects related to business and industry on the part of library staff;
- Few requests for business-related materials or online databases.

The attitudes and perceptions of administrators and library professional staff that result in minimal or irregular promotional programs contribute to the lack of adequate funding and support to provide the services and resources that should be available to the business community. A consistent and concentrated effort to gain the attention, cooperation, and allegiance of businesspeople should empower public libraries to provide full access to information and technologies.

The imposition of fees for certain services no doubt places a barrier between certain members of the public and information resources they need. For example, the young person who needs something photocopied or lent from another library, or information on a database, cannot fulfill his need if he does not have the money. The fee versus free debate, particularly in public libraries, will probably continue until the costs of such expensive services as online database searching, electronic document delivery, and telefascimile are reduced to a level at which it is possible to offer them to all searchers free of charge, or until library budgets increase to a point where fees for services are no longer necessary, thus effectively killing the debate. Neither of these solutions seem likely in the foreseeable future. Public library costs continue to rise as budgets fall, and more libraries retain traditional fees and add new ones. The list of client charges, based on the survey responses and the author's other research and experience, includes the following:

- Short loan "rental" charges for new titles on best seller lists;
- Reserve processing, postage and handling fees;
- Postage and handling for books-by-mail service;
- Lost library cards;
- Use of films, videos, records, compact discs—including damage insurance pre-payment fees;
- Fines for overdue materials;
- Use of meeting rooms;
- Interlibrary loan service, including additional charges for obtaining materials from outside sources;
- Photocopies;
- Online database searching—printing results, paper used, off-line printouts, online time, telecommunications charges, per-hour charges for searching, staff time/research surcharges;
- CD-ROM paper use;
- Document delivery, including postal, fax, courier service charges;
- Staff research time for manual and/or automated searching and special in-depth research projects;
- Membership fees or library-use charges for non-residents;
- Telephone reference service through installation of a 900 number.

The common defense for these fees is that they are essential to the provision of services due to the deadly combination of decreased budgets and high inflation rates. Other reasons given include:

- Poor administrative support and minimal funding allotted to support totally or partially free automated information retrieval systems, rapid document delivery, cooperative network membership, adequate staff and training programs;
- Fees provide an additional source of income;
- Full cost recovery allows access to expensive computerized systems;
- Fees limit service to serious users (whoever they are) and prevent frivolous use (however this is defined);
- Charges increase appreciation and respect for "serious" computer-based resources;
- Charges limit access according to the budget available for online information retrieval;
- Fees encourage the use of less expensive manual resources before turning to online databases, even though the databases are more up-to-date and efficient;
- Telephone reference and fax fees discourage "lazy" clients from taking up librarians' time reading to them or doing their research.

Some of the reasons for charging for services seem to show a bias against technology as well as service to remote users. They seem destructive to library service, because business clients frequently need on-the-spot information for important and immediate decisions, however "serious" or "frivolous" they may appear to be.

If a library administration argues that it is essential to charge fees, the reasons for imposing them should be carefully examined. They make sense if they represent the only way to meet the demand for free, unrestricted access to a greater variety of data. Indeed, "free" does not only mean free of charge. If the library does not make available a full range of services and resources because it cannot afford the cost, then access is denied regardless of clients' information needs or their ability to pay. Charging fees, or developing special fee-based services, allows patrons to get what is necessary within their own budgetary limitations, by using affordable services and resources with costs attached, or the "free" hard copy collection.

Professionals who may be totally against charging fees because they are unshakably committed to the philosophy of free access as a right to all taxpayers tend not to voice objections to a variety of service restrictions, also imposed free of charge, that can seriously affect the quality of public library service, and make the library less attractive for fulfilling information needs. These restrictions include the following:

- Staff and time limitations for both telephoning and visiting patrons;
- No call-backs allowed;
- A limit to the number of questions allowed per call or visit;

- No directory information, no extensive research, no online searching prior to exhausting manual resources;
- Online searching is limited by time spent, or is available only at the discretion of the librarian;
- Online searching is restricted by the number of citations, abstracts, or full-text articles printed;
- Use of CD-ROMs is limited by time used per patron;
- No photocopying by staff is permitted;
- Fax service is not available or not encouraged;
- No referrals to other libraries are made;
- Access to certain services is by appointment only;
- Use is restricted to city, county, or district residents;
- Curtailed library hours—including no evenings, Saturdays or Sundays;
- Limited hours for access to special services, such as online database searching, placing interlibrary loan requests, and document delivery.

These and similar limitations, certainly do not enhance the public library image as a vital community institution, assisting the economic development of business and industry as an information provider. So the question remains—to charge, or not to charge.

Clearly, quality information and reference service to the business community is affected by staff motivation, attitudes related to "catering" to the business community, and interest in the subject area. Unfortunately, many libraries lack one or more of the following:

- Professionals with special knowledge of manual and automated business resources;
- Those who are willing to expend the extra energy needed to keep up-to-date with resources within and outside of the library;
- Developers of solid business collections that target community needs;
- Planners and implementers of promotional and training programs;
- Liaison personnel to go out into the community to get to know local businesspeople;
- And those who would vigorously engage in the marketing of library services to gain political and financial support and funding to make state-of-the-art services possible.

Libraries need to cooperate with one another in order to knock down barriers and make full access to all resources and services possible. Creating links among public, corporate, academic, association, and other special libraries ensures that the resources and services available in one library, will be supplemented by those in other libraries. Cooperation includes staff knowledge of what other libraries have to offer, as well as sharing materials via interlibrary loan or direct access by telephone, fax, electronic mail, or an in-person visit.

Staff shortages have impacted workloads, while technology has caused an increase in the variety of work to be done. Since staffing levels are either static or shrinking, informal informational networks, as well as memberships in formal cooperative networks, are advantageous for knocking down barriers to data not accessible in a client's local library. Journal articles, and other materials outside the main subject interest of a corporate library, are within reach via resource sharing. So, corporate librarians should view public library services as value-added, when there is a need for special data not directly related to corporate goals. In contrast, public libraries should approach their corporate, academic, and special library neighbors in order to increase their success rates.

Since the majority of businesses in the country are small ones, public libraries can greatly enhance service by creating cooperative links with non-library organizations that exist to provide assistance to small businesses. The U.S. Small Business Association offers such programs as advocacy, financial assistance, procurement (government contracts) assistance, minority small business development, counseling and training by SCORE (Service Corps of Retired Executives) volunteers, while Chambers of Commerce provide demographic and community economic information, advocacy, training, and more. These organizations often serve as library advocates and referral agencies. Also, librarians can attract more small business personnel, entrepreneurs, and job seekers by arranging for programs, sponsored by these agencies, to be conveniently held in the local library.

The need for greater resource sharing is as evident as budget cuts and library downsizing, but the most significant barrier to the development of stronger cooperative links is also insufficient funding.

Public libraries must keep up with economic changes and community business and industry trends—responding to them by identifying and adding the resources and services needed to make access to information easier and more efficient. Without an enlightened administration to provide the necessary incentives, free and open access will remain a philosophical ideal.

2

Public Library Business Information and Reference Service: An Overview of Present Activity

When investigating current trends and alternative approaches to the development, maintenance, and expansion of service to business, an overview of present activity in libraries is essential. From such an overview may come the discovery of current attitudes, philosophies, the extent of service, and the level of emphasis placed on the use of automated systems as a means of increasing the quality and quantity of the reference and information product for the business client. For this purpose one hundred questionnaires were sent by this author to public libraries and one hundred to corporate libraries in large urban areas, and adjacent suburban cities throughout the United States. It was hoped that geographically related public and corporate libraries would respond so that direct comparisons of service might be obtained. Out of one hundred possible pairs, only thirty-four were identified. The data received from these library pairs were not uniquely different from those of the other respondents.

In order to increase the size of the sample, all state librarians and all Special Libraries Association chapter officers were asked to duplicate the questionnaire and send it to two or three librarians in their states or chapters. Many of them were quite enthusiastic about the topic of the questionnaire—some even went considerably beyond what was asked of them by offering excellent suggestions and valuable information to enhance the study. A number of corporate librarians did not respond, perhaps due to the proprietary nature of their libraries. But this relatively small sample (79) of the entire universe of corporate libraries provides an overview of corporate library activity that is consistent with profiles available in the literature. The higher return rate from public libraries (124) gives a somewhat better picture of business information and reference service activity, but it too is not a big enough sample to apply the findings to the population at large. The value of the data lies in the fact that they serve as a way of comparing and contrasting levels of information and reference service practices and cooperative efforts in public and corporate libraries located in areas showing significant business activity. The geographical spread of the survey sample reflects the range of library business activity in the United States, as seen in the following table:

Summary of Locations of Responding Libraries by Region/State

	Number of Public	Number of Corporate
North East:		
Connecticut	5	4
Delaware	2	0
District of Columbia	1	1
Maine	1	0
Maryland	4	0
Massachusetts	7	4
New Hampshire	3	0
New Jersey	9	4
New York	7	3
Pennsylvania	3	5
Totals: 10 States	42	21
North West:		
Idaho	1	1
Montana	1	0
Oregon	1	1
Washington	2	3
Totals: 4 States	5	5
Midwest:		
Illinois	5	7
Indiana	2	1
Iowa	8	0
Kansas	0	1
Nebraska	1	1
Ohio	4	5
South Dakota	2	0
Totals: 7 States	22	15

	Number of Public	Number of Corporate
South East:		
Alabama	2	2
Florida	4	1
Georgia	3	1
Louisiana	4	3
Mississippi	1	0
South Carolina	2	0
Tennessee	0	2
Virginia	1	0
West Virginia	4	0
Totals: 9 States	21	9
West:		
California	8	9
Nevada	1	0
Utah	3	0
Totals: 3 States	12	9
South West:		
Arizona	0	3
New Mexico	0	1
North Carolina	2	0
Oklahoma	2	1
Texas	3	2
Totals: 5 States	7	7
Pacific:		
Hawaii	1	1
Totals: 1 State	1	1
Central:		
Missouri	1	3
Totals: 1 State	*1*	*3*
North Central:		
Wisconsin	4	1
Michigan	6	2
Minnesota	1	4
North Dakota	1	0
Totals: 4 States	12	7
East Central:		
Kentucky	1	2
Totals: 1 State	1	2
Grand Total: (45 States)	124	79

RESPONDENTS

Of the 100 questionnaires sent directly to public libraries, selected from the American Library Association's directory when a corporate library was listed for the same geographical area, 77 responded. Forty-seven questionnaires sent via 26 state librarians were returned—nine responses came from one state, four from another, and six states returned three each. Of the total of 124 public libraries, 36 are located in large urban areas (34% in the North East), while the rest serve smaller cities.

General Information

The organizational mode typical to 36 out of 124 of the libraries surveyed is that of a business center located in the main library of large urban systems. Separate business collections strategically located in or near the business district, while the ideal, is not common. Small- and medium-sized libraries tend to integrate business resources within the entire collection since space and staffing mandate this arrangement. The following table shows the variety of arrangements described:

Percentage	(number of libraries)	Type of Arrangement
83%	103	Business information center located in the main library
10%	13	Business collection integrated with the reference collection with general reference department staff providing service
3%	4	Separate business library located in or near the business district
1%	1	Separate specialized center in development
1%	1	Business information center in a branch library in a system with no main library
1%	1	Library located in central business district with business reference sources integrated with general reference collection
1%	1	A combined business and technology division in the main library

Although 86% (107) libraries have professional staff available to provide business reference and information service on evenings and 88% (109) on Saturdays, 52% (64 libraries,) mostly those located in smaller cities, do not have Sunday hours. Ten libraries (8%) are not open on Sundays in the summer months; some are open only some evenings per week, just one per month in one case. One librarian commented that the library used to be open one evening, but due to cutbacks, this was eliminated. Full seven day service is not a common trend due to lack of sufficient funding and necessary staff.

Eighty-one librarians (65%) reported that job seekers use the business and information service most frequently—not surprising because of the current rate of unemployment. The increase in urban and suburban entrepreneurship and cottage industry is reflected by the fact that this group ranks second in usage. In light of this author's research and experience, it is not surprising to find that corporate library staff, researchers, and technicians use public libraries infrequently. They are either not aware of accessible resources or they use other types of libraries or services to obtain information not available in their own collections. The specifics about the nature of the various user types can be seen in the following table:

Frequency of Use of the Business and Information Service by Various User Groups

Ranking: Least 1 2 3 4 5 Most

User Groups	Number of Libraries				
	1	2	3	4	5
Corporate personnel	36	25	25	21	14
Personnel of small- or medium-sized businesses	7	10	32	34	38
Entrepreneurs or self-employed	3	7	18	48	45
Researchers or technicians	34	33	39	13	2
Government officials	39	26	34	12	10
Corporate library staff	63	24	13	16	5
Academic library staff	81	26	7	3	4
Job seekers	5	5	15	15	81
Students	10	11	22	43	35
Special interest groups	64	19	22	11	5
Investors	0	2	2	4	5
Consumers	0	2	0	0	5
Legal and accounting firms	0	0	0	0	2
Non-profit organization Staff/volunteers	0	0	0	0	1
Unions	0	0	0	1	0

Note: 3 libraries did not answer the question.

THE COLLECTION

The business information and reference collections of all of the survey libraries (100%) include dictionaries and encyclopedias. The majority of the respondents also have subject specific indexes (90%), government documents (84%), company reports and corporate data (90%), industry data, statistics, and trends (92%), general newspapers and journals (89%), subject and industry-specific newspapers and journals (73%), local and state regulations and reports (70], legal indexes, dictionaries, and encyclopedias (64%), and employment and occupation resources (92%). Newspaper clipping files and newsletters are available in 53% of the libraries. Patent and trademark data are available in 49% of the responding libraries. Only 11 large urban libraries provide access to doctoral dissertations and theses.

Quite a variety of other resources are available in one or two business collections. These include:

• Corporate and trade directories
• General and subject-specific directories
• Listings of standards/specifications/codes
• Industrial and military standards
• Government documents, such as local and state regulations and reports
• Stock market information
• Telephone directories
• General and local newspapers
• Newspaper index for local companies
• Tax and career information
• Investment tools, economics, marketing, public relations, real estate, labor relations, management, production and research, business communication and writing sources
• Mail order catalogs
• Real estate service—maps, sales reports
• File of local business contacts, i.e. small business development center
• Consumer information sources
• Job service—for example, listings of available positions

The last three resources listed are available in small libraries actively engaged in increasing use for business purposes. The case studies give profiles of the scope and depth of use of such resources.

SERVICES

A wide array of services are available in the responding libraries, but those dependent on electronic systems are less common. Large urban libraries that serve a significant business clientele tend to acquire the most efficient and varied services, since they tend to obtain the funding to support such services. The increased importance of electronic media to boost efficiency presents a problem for the libraries that do not add value via online database searching, electronic document delivery, updating service (SDI), telefascimile, and more.

All but three libraries (96%) provide interlibrary loan service for items not in the collection. That all public libraries would not use interlibrary loans to obtain items not in the collection is puzzling.

Two librarians mentioned the method of processing requests. In one case, they are routed to the ILL department from a special business branch in a downtown urban area, and in another, from the main library business department of a county system.

The majority of the respondents (96%) have ready-reference series (including photocopy). Telephone reference service is available for business information and reference users in 118 (95%) of the cases. Ninety-three libraries (75%) retrieve hard-to-find or obscure information, while 90 (73%) have available mediated online database searching (librarian searches). These libraries represent a fairly even mix of those in large urban areas and smaller cities.

The growing importance of telefascimile service to business clients is somewhat evident in that 74 (60%) of the respondents reported its availability in their libraries.

Training programs on business resources, the use of the collection, and end-user searching are common to only 51 (41%) libraries. One might assume from this finding that the primary need of business clients continues to be the traditional "information in a hurry." Many of them do not have the time or inclination to learn retrieval skills, but there might be insufficient staff to plan for or implement such programs.

Only 31 libraries (25%) court the business community by providing bibliographies of new items in the field. Fifteen (12%) provide SDI service (Selective Dissemination of Information) or monthly updates on specific topics, including bibliographic data and abstracts, while end-user searching of online or CD-ROM databases (patron searches) and editing of downloaded search results prior to delivery in printed or electronic formats is available in just 12 (10%) libraries.

Other services mentioned are:

Percentage	(number of libraries)	Type of Service
10%	12	CD-ROMs available for patron searching, downloading, and printing
2%	2	In-library programs and presentations at business group meetings
1%	1	Staff-created in-house databases
1%	1	Local clipping vertical file
2%	2	Business reference card/pass for the use of the collections of other libraries
1%	1	Books and audio-visual materials available by mail

Service Restrictions

There is no pattern to service restrictions that is based on the size or location of the individual libraries, but the variety is staggering and a disappointing trend. Twelve libraries (10%) reported no restrictions on services provided to the business community, except those of staff availability and time limitations. This fact is problematic because the extent or type of limitations caused by staff or time shortages is not defined. Verbatim comments on the question of service limitations suggest that restrictions are universal even though policy states that there are none:

> "Presently there are no restrictions, but there is a plan to implement time limitations soon since business clients are increasing, while staffing has not."

> Service in one large urban library is "only limited by the copyright law and the knowledge and expertise of the staff."

> "There is no time limit on questions unless the patron specifies one—the time spent per question varies from up to an hour or more, depending on available staff time." Rather than using limited staffing as a reason for restricting service, this library pays attention to all queries received—using call-backs for many questions when necessary. Fax service is, however, limited to ten pages locally and four pages long distance.

> "A philosophy of "we can" rather than "we can't." is promoted. As a result, library policy contains few restrictions. An attempt is made to answer each question as thoroughly as possible. Librarians learn to juggle the people waiting in line with the callers on the telephone, so call-backs are frequent."

"Business librarians are readily willing to meet individually with patrons requiring assistance, and put themselves personally at the disposal of any business client who telephones or visits the library. There is usually no limit to the amount of time it takes to answer a business question if staff is not serving at the general reference desk. In addition, the staff is willing to look for information and arrange to call the patron back at a later time."

A number of other librarians reported that limitations are determined by the best judgment of professional staff with regard to calling a patron back or suggesting that the patron come in to the library.

Ninety-seven respondents (78%) listed a variety of common service restrictions mostly applicable to telephoning patrons, evidence of the negative perception that telephoning patrons are less important that those visiting the library. Some of the limitations specified include the following:

- No limitations are placed on in-person service, but some are placed on telephone service—no extensive student research is done over the telephone; no nearby information from the city directory or the criss-cross directory is checked; consumer evaluations are not given; legal and medical questions are not answered if they require interpretation (the staff searches for answers, but asks patrons to come in and study what was found, thereby making their own interpretation); depending on how busy the librarians are, they might limit the number of addresses read per phone call (this number is flexible).
- No criss-cross directory information or stock quotations are given out over the telephone. An attempt is made to retrieve hard-to-find or obscure information as time permits, but in most cases the patron is asked to come in for help with searching.
- There is a three minute, three question limit on telephone reference, but if a question takes more than three minutes to answer, the patron's name and telephone number is taken for a call back.
- Call-backs are done only in extreme situations—for example, overseas or out-of-state replies; two questions per telephone call are allowed with a time limitation of two to four minutes per call. Questions answered include company address and telephone number, stock quotes, other ready-reference business information.
- Limitations are determined by the best judgment of the professional staff with regard to calling a patron back or suggesting that the patron come in to the library.
- Long, detailed telephoned information requests are not answered; rather, patrons are encouraged to come in for instruction on how to find the information.

- Telephone reference questions are not accepted if the patron cannot provide a call-back number.
- A limit of three is usually used: three company names and addresses, three stock quotes, etc. If the department is not busy, more than three items are checked.
- There is a time restriction of fifteen to twenty minutes per question. Three stock quotes, or three car value figures per caller per day are provided.
- Only five addresses are looked up over the phone; no long distance call-backs are allowed.
- Only six directory-type questions are accepted per call.
- The ready-reference time limitation is five-ten minutes and there is a maximum of thirty minutes allowed for call-backs (local area only.) Three questions are accepted per call. Indexes are not searched, bibliographies are not provided, and no consumer product evaluations are given over the phone.
- Telephone reference is restricted to three fact questions or five minutes; call-backs are avoided if possible; the librarians prefer to handle questions when the caller is on the line.
- Phone calls are limited to five minutes, and up to one hour is spent on call-backs.
- Three items are looked up at a time over the telephone, but no more than twenty-five pages are faxed at one time.
- There is a five minute time limitation on telephone reference and approximately thirty minutes on walk-ins.
- No call-backs are made; five minutes are allowed for telephone queries, and five-ten minutes for in-person questions.
- No long distance call-backs are allowed—the patron must call again; faxes are sent only to libraries, not to individuals or businesses.
- Librarians are encouraged to take down lengthy reference questions in order to call the patrons back with answers; medical and legal questions are not answered, except to cite directly from sources.
- No photocopying is done by the staff for patrons; no in-depth research is performed and then presented to patrons.
- No in-depth research is done, i.e., gathering together resources for a student's term paper, doing extensive patent searching. These more extensive queries are referred to the fee-based service.
- Five obvious sources are checked. If information is not readily available, patrons are invited to do their own research with staff assistance. If patrons want research done for them, they are referred to the fee-based service.
- In-library use only is permitted because most business material does not circulate.
- Interlibrary loan is offered only to city residents and businesses.

- Photocopying is limited to ten pages maximum; fax service is only available as an exception with the department head's approval—it is not offered or encouraged.
- There is a limitation of fifteen minutes per question with referral to reference network available.
- Patrons are limited to five interlibrary loan requests at one time; fax is limited to up to twenty pages.
- Time limitations are imposed on the use of certain reference materials—from thirty minutes to an hour; city directory assistance is given for specific addresses only; identification for many reference items must be held while the patron uses them because of a theft problem.
- Reference/research is limited to one hour per question; if a librarian thinks a particular request will take too much time, the patron is referred to known public or private sources.

In order to ensure that all types of information, regardless of topic or source, is delivered to business clients, 92 (74%) libraries refer patrons from the business information and reference service to other departments of the main library for answers to questions covering other subject areas. Those that do not do so are seven (6%) small libraries with integrated collections. This result presents problems because too many patrons may not be directed to alternative information sources within the library.

Marketing Service

Eighty-four survey respondents (68%) recognize the importance of actively marketing business information and reference service, and 60 (71%) primarily use the most inexpensive promotional formats—bookmarks, flyers, and posters. These are effective media. But combining them with more energetic marketing strategies may better demonstrate the value of the public library to businesspeople. Other methods include the following:

Percentage	(number of libraries)	Promotional Media
70%	59	Subject bibliographies
54%	45	Library newsletter
52%	44	Newspaper ads/articles
50%	42	Exhibits at business/industry fairs and conventions
29%	24	Radio/television
27%	23	Lists of new acquisition

Continued

Percentage	(number of libraries)	Promotional Media
19%	16	Special fee-based research service for corporate personnel
13%	11	Direct mail campaigns
8%	7	Library tours, talks at off-site locations, in-house seminars and workshops for career services and outplacement agencies, as well as programs on a variety of topics, for example, financing, small businesses, marketing techniques, patent searching and registration, and investment information
6%	5	Training programs held at other libraries; presentations at various government agencies, and forums given at the Small Business Association and the Chamber of Commerce
2%	2	Business librarians actively serve in business organizations in the community
2%	2	Monthly business breakfast, including a discussion of the contents of the collection and how to use it
2%	2	Columns published regularly (monthly, weekly) or irregularly in the library system newsletter and in other business newsletters
1%	1	Weekly program series and talks at local business organizations; presentations to business groups and college business management classes
1%	1	Business department program listings in the local newspaper

In summary, libraries are using a variety of promotional aids to attract new users, friends, and potential supporters from the business community. Clearly many of the different approaches require a great deal of effort, commitment, and administrative support, along with an appreciation of the value of library service to the business community, and the significance of the library's role as an information provider.

COOPERATION AND CORPORATE LIBRARIES

Cooperation among libraries is essential to ensure total access to all resources and information needed by the business community. Of the 124 responding libraries, 94% (116) cooperate with at least one other public library. Other cooperative relationships are as follows:

Percentage	(number of libraries)	Type of Library
88%	109	College and university
64%	79	Corporate
32%	40	Association
28%	35	Special (medical, state, institutional, elementary/secondary school, newspaper, government, law, etc.)

Whether or not any cooperative links were established in five of the responding libraries (4%) is unknown, since no indication of any relationships with other libraries was given.

Cooperation with corporate libraries invites special attention, and respondents provided specifics about the nature of their cooperative relationship, as seen in the following table:

Table of Frequency of Requests of Resources from Corporate Libraries to Public Libraries

Ranking: Least 1   2   3   4   5 Most

Resources	Number of Libraries				
	1	2	3	4	5
Books or monographs related to individual requests not available in your library	37	9	13	14	9
Articles from journals not available in your library	18	7	14	13	30
Data on particular corporations	46	10	7	8	11
Information on research findings in a particular industry or corporation	51	10	8	7	6
Medical, legal or technical research data	45	8	13	7	9
Special indexes, bibliographies, or dictionaries	58	10	7	1	6
Government documents or reports	51	9	10	6	6

Continued

Resources	Number of Libraries				
	1	2	3	4	5
Online databases not available in your library or not searched	66	6	5	1	4
CD-ROM databases not available in your library	71	3	6	1	1
Standards or specifications	0	0	0	1	4
Investment resources	0	0	0	0	1
Specific information regarding the particular corporation or industry	0	0	0	0	1
Updated issues of expensive services for which we have older or sample issues	0	0	0	0	2
Occasional conference proceedings	0	0	1	0	0
Newspaper search	0	0	1	0	0
Legal material	0	0	1	0	0

Journal articles not available in the public library are most frequently requested from corporate libraries. Data on specific corporations, and books or monographs related to individual requests and not available in the public library are less frequent, but still important requests. Electronic resources, e.g., online databases and CD-ROM databases, are the least frequently requested resources. Other resources which public libraries frequently access through corporate library partners include the following:

• Standards
• Specifications
• Investment resources
• Corporation or industry-specific data
• Conference proceedings
• Newspapers
• Legal material

In most cases the partnership includes patron referral. Sixty-nine (56%) public libraries refer patrons directly to the cooperating corporate library, providing them with the name, location, and library hours (46 libraries) or prearranging the patron visit (23 libraries.) In other cases, referrals are made by using one or more of the following methods, depending on the client's preference and the urgency of the need for the information:

- The librarian calls the referral library to explain the request
- The librarian obtains information from the corporate library and delivers it to the patron
- The corporate library is called and asked to send the information to the patron
- The library is called to determine what sources are available
- A pass is issued to patrons for access to the corporate library
- The librarian calls to obtain permission for the patron to use specific materials in the corporate library

Verbatim comments on the question of referrals indicate that some cooperative links are tentative, but significant enough to merit attention. These include the following:

Most of the corporate libraries rely on us (public library) to fulfill information requests.

No referrals are made to corporate libraries, but occasionally we call the corporate librarian for help to photocopy some missing pages from a service.

Referrals are rarely made—we just use corporate libraries for interlibrary loan.

Referrals are made only if the SLA Directory indicates the corporate library's willingness to cooperate.

Most corporate libraries impose a mix of service limitations on the patrons who are referred to them. The limitations include the following:

- No on-site visits; interlibrary loan only
- Advance permission required for referral
- On-site use only
- No photocopying
- Time limitations
- Access allowed only one day per week
- Access limited to non-proprietary data
- Appointment required
- Notification of the nature of the request required

Restrictions vary and depend upon the individual corporate library policies regarding use by the general public. One librarian stated that the local corporate libraries are closed to the public, but limitations are circumvented by a staff member who has a friend in one corporate library and was employed by another.

Cooperation with corporate libraries has increased in 18 libraries (23%) in the past and present fiscal years. The reasons for increased cooperation are typically the need for reference resources not available in the public library, or membership in cooperative networks. Half of these 18 libraries found the need for corporate library reference resources grew due to the demand for a greater variety of journals identified through online database searching. Other reasons for increased cooperation include:

- Inadequate budget coupled with the rising cost of materials
- Information needs are rapidly and thoroughly filled by corporate libraries
- Corporate library listings in directories
- Personal contact with corporate librarians at professional and business meetings
- Corporate librarians are former business department employees

In one case cooperation increased because corporate libraries increased their use of public library services, particularly for searching online business databases and for gaining access to government publications, historical data, and other specialized sources unique to the collection. In this case, and possibly in many others, the special information needs of corporate personnel have led to closer ties with public library business collections. This may be an important step toward greater public and corporate library reciprocation and the development of new public-corporate partnerships.

ELECTRONIC SERVICES

Using CD-ROM products as a cost-effective way of supplementing the hard copy collection with more recent data is valued by 76% (94) of the survey respondents. Large urban libraries tend to have a greater variety of these databases—in three libraries patrons may access ten or more, and six others have an assortment of from five to seven different CD-ROM products.

InfoTrac is the product of choice for 90 libraries (96%). Most provide access to the *InfoTrac General Business File* (includes *Investext*), while some respondents listed the *General Periodicals and Newspaper Index* and *Magazine Index Plus* as well. Seven libraries also have *IAC (Information Access Company) Company Profiles*. The *Health Reference Center* is available in six libraries. Other CD-ROM databases listed are as follows:

Percentage   (number of libraries)   Database

Percentage	(number of libraries)	Database
28%	26	*Compact Disclosure*
24%	23	*ABI/INFORM*
20%	19	*NTIB (National Trade Data Bank)*
14%	13	*U.S. Census*
12%	11	*CASSIS & Trademarks from U.S. Patent and Trademark Office*
12%	11	*MARCIVE (Government Publications Index)*
10%	9	*CIRR (now defunct)*
10%	9	*Dun's MIllion Dollar Disc*
6%	6	*Standard & Poor's Corporations*
6%	6	*U.S. Imports of Merchandise & U.S. Exports of Merchandise*
5%	5	*National Economic, Social & Environmental Databank*
5%	5	*Business Abstracts*
5%	5	*Dun's Business Locator*
5%	5	*Business Newsbank*
4%	4	*Thomas Register*
4%	4	*American Business Disk*
4%	4	*Predicasts F&S U.S. & International*
3%	3	*Business Dateline*
2%	2	*Wilsondisc databases*
2%	2	*D&B Market Identifiers*
2%	2	*Books in Print*
2%	2	*Hazardous Materials Information System*
1%	1	*ABI Business Periodicals on Disc*
1%	1	*Moody's*
1%	1	*Mutual Funds on Disc*
1%	1	*Proquest Magazine Index*

The survey results show that online databases have a 2% lead over CD-ROM as the electronic source of choice, a hint of the decline in popularity of the less efficient CD-ROM databases due to a number of factors—for example, serious time lags, format and software problems. Ninety-seven libraries (78%) offer online search services—with 54 (56%) subscribing to two or more systems. A comparison of the vendor systems available reveals that location (in terms of population density) is not a factor in the decision to make automated information retrieval available to the business community.

Eighty-six (89%) of the libraries subscribe to *DIALOG,* with its wide variety of databases; it is the most popular system. Online access to full-text newspapers was not lost when *VU/TEXT* was phased out and most of the files transferred over to *DIALOG,* because the 26 subscribers (27%) also access *DIALOG.*

Only 32 libraries (33%) search *Wilsonline,* while 23 (24%) of the survey respondents subscribe to *BRS.* Even fewer libraries provide access to other vendor systems as follows:

Percentage	(number of libraries)	Vender System
16%	16	*Dow Jones News Retrieval*
14%	14	*DataTimes*
12%	12	*NEXIS*
9%	9	*EPIC (OCLC)*
7%	7	*ORBIT*
4%	4	*NewsNet*
3%	3	*LOGIN (Local Government Information Network*
3%	3	*Easynet*
2%	3	*CompuServe*
2%	2	*Westlaw*

In four cases, access to online databases is available via state or regional networks. One large urban library refers clients to the online search service in the general reference department. The request is then forwarded to a regional network. Three small city libraries interview the patron, and send the written statement to the state network.

Budgetary constraints resulted in the reduction of vendor systems from eight to just one (*DataTimes*) in one library, and from five to one (*DIALOG*) in another. Both of these libraries are located in large urban areas with quite varied business clientele. The need to narrow the availability of databases, often unique to a particular system, markedly reduces the quality of service to the business community.

The databases most frequently searched cover subjects of high interest to the business community. Of those specified, *ABI/Inform* is most frequently used by 57 libraries (59%). Forty-two of the survey respondents (43%) search *PTS Prompt* often, while 40 (41%) use *Trademarkscan,* and 37 (38%) search *D&B Dun's Financial Records.* Other high use databases are *Trade & Industry Index* (34%), *D&B Donnelly Demographics* (28%), *Management Contents* (27%), *Business Dateline* (19%), and *CENDATA* (18%). *Business Periodicals Index* and *PAIS International* are heavily used by 16% of those surveyed.

At least one, and as many as 12 librarians (1%-12%) indicated that they frequently search the following databases:

- *American Banker Full Text*
- *BioBusiness*
- *Business Software Database*
- *Chemical Industry Notes*
- *Disclosure/Spectrum Ownership*
- *Foods Adlibra*
- *Health Planning and Administration*
- *Investext*
- *Labordoc*
- *Pharmaceutical News Index*
- *Standard & Poors News*
- *DIALOG/VU/TEXT/DataTimes full-text newspapers files*
- *Claims Patents*
- *DIALOG Company Name Finder*
- *Medline*
- *Dun's Market Identifiers (National/International)*
- *Kompass*
- *Dun's Million Dollar Directory*
- *Federal Register*
- *DIALOG international databases*
- *D&B Electronic Business Directory*
- *Trinet*
- *Westlaw databases*
- *ERIC*

One librarian commented that no record of databases used is kept, but this will probably change in the future; the reason for this change is not explained. Without formal tracking of what is searched there can be no evaluation of patron satisfaction, effectiveness of staff training, costs, and other factors.

Limitations placed on online database searching for business persons effect the quality, quantity, and efficiency of business information and reference service, along with the degree of client satisfaction. Nevertheless, limitations exist in most public libraries, particularly for those that have insufficient funding, and/or poor administrative support to provide free or partially free service. Charges and time limitations continue to be the most frequent restrictions imposed on public library clients.

Eighty-two (86%) of the 97 libraries that have online searching listed limitations:

Percentage	(number of libraries)	Limitations
73%	49	Charges
26%	21	Time spent on the search
10%	8	Number of citations printed
6%	5	Number of full text records printed
5%	4	Number of abstracts with citations printed
2%	2	Number of databases searched

With the exception of one library, where the patron's own cost limitation is the only consideration, other restrictions narrow the scope of service considerably. In addition to those listed in the table above, a number of survey respondents listed the following limitations:

- All print/CD-ROM sources must be exhausted first.
- No on-demand online searching is done; searches are conducted with the discretion of the librarian as part of reference service.
- No full-text of articles are retrieved; the patron is referred to interlibrary loan.
- To control online searching activity, an interview is required; the search is completed within three days of the request.
- For other than ready-reference searching, an appointment with the librarian is required.
- One search per month per patron is allowed, with a minimum of 30 minutes spent searching paper or other available sources. The request must involve Boolean concepts. No printouts from directories are allowed.
- Free service for five minutes of searching time and 20 records is available.

When asked if limitations would be waived for corporate personnel willing to pay full cost (including staff time) for in-depth research, monthly updates (SDI) on specific topic(s), 25 librarians (30%) responded affirmatively. This kind of flexibility is an acknowledgement of the practical necessity of accommodating the special needs of businesspersons in order to provide quality library service.

Limitations placed on requests for in-depth research are usually not waived because of rigid policy, insufficient staff to accommodate clients with lengthy search requests, or the existence of a fee-based service either in-house, or in another library. One library routinely refers such requests to two commercial information brokers.

Charging public library patrons for online searching has been a topic of great controversy for years. Fees are often justified if they are used to subsidize a service fully or partially when the budget is limited. However, this practice is condemned by many professionals who believe that charging for service represents a double tax, a way of restricting access of information to those who can afford to pay, and that it is illegal when imposed by a free public institution. Nevertheless, 67% of the surveyed libraries (65) reported policies that include charges. The practices specified usually allow for some free searching, providing at least some "special" service to all clients. The fees range from $5.00 to full cost, and sometimes include charges for librarian time. The practices listed include the following:

- First ten minutes free, and then $1.25 per minute after.
- $25.00 per hour for librarian time and full cost of the online search.
- The library picks up the first $5.00.
- Free up to $15.00 for city residents.
- $30.00 per hour plus the cost of the search.
- There is no charge for anything up to ten minutes or $10.00.
- A fee-based search is limited to $250.00.
- No charge for the librarian's time but the patron must pay online and connect-time charges.
- Patron must pay for connect time, printing charges, and a library service charge of $6.00 per 15 minutes spent searching (or $24.00 an hour plus tax.)
- $15.00 an hour plus actual online charges.
- $5.00 plus online charges.
- Free up to $10.00, and then full cost.
- Free for ready!reference searches, otherwise $75.00 an hour and online costs.
- Free up to the discretion of the staff ($20.00-$30.00), then full cost.
- Patron is charged for connect time, telecommunications time and print charges.
- Free up to $5.00; then full cost plus 10% plus $5.00 per search.
- Quick reference charges are sometimes absorbed according to professional judgment and the situation. Otherwise, the patron is charged full cost as calculated by databases at the end of the search plus online and other printcharges.
- $30.00 per month free for patron; any searches above $30.00, the patron is charged $10.00 per search.
- $25.00 per hour for the librarian's time, plus the database charges, with a $15.00 minimum charge.
- Ten minutes free, and then $1.50 per minute.

- The library pays the first $7.50 of a search and the patron pays the balance.
- Searches are free up to $30.00. If the cost is greater than that, it is referred to the library system's information clearinghouse. They determine the total estimated cost and will search for free on a case-by-case basis. If the charges exceed our willingness to search for free, the patron is referred to a commercial fee-based service.
- The patron is charged full cost plus a 10% surcharge.
- Free up to $10.00 for county residents; out-of-county residents pay the full cost of the search.

In summary, the charging practices listed are as varied as the points made in arguing against them. Presumably, the librarians that provide some or all searching for a fee have reasonable defenses, the most powerful one being the inability to provide any online searching without passing the costs on to the patrons.

NETWORKS AND INTERLIBRARY LOAN

Membership in networks is essential for resource sharing and efficient document delivery for all member libraries. This ensures the availability of information that is not otherwise accessible. Of the 124 survey participants, 91% (113) participate in at least one network, as follows:

Percentage	(number of libraries)	Networks
81%	91	OCLC
74%	84	State, regional, metropolitan regional and local area networks
4%	5	RLIN
4%	5	WLN
4%	5	UTLAS
4%	4	Michigan Library Consortium

Since only a few survey libraries are members of RLIN, the Michigan Library Consortium, WLN and UTLAS, these networks are not significant for resource sharing and document delivery.

Even though ten librarians (10%) did not answer the question, one might assume that some sort of networking activity is present. It is difficult to believe that these libraries (located in both large urban areas and small cities) successfully serve their clients without outside help.

The business collection is most frequently supplemented through the use of interlibrary loan to obtain non-current periodicals, resources in other related subject fields, and obscure or scholarly periodicals. Government documents and company or industry data are somewhat significant, but requests for dissertations or theses are minimal.

Interlibrary loan service is of particular importance to some libraries, and respondents provided specifics about the nature of their activity, as seen in the following table:

Significance of Resources to Interlibrary Loan Use
for Supplementing the Public Library Business Collection

Ranking: Least 1 2 3 4 5 Most

Resources	Number of Libraries				
	1	2	3	4	5
Resources in other related subject fields	31	11	22	18	26
Obscure/scholarly periodicals	48	5	15	17	23
Dissertations or theses	77	13	11	4	5
Non-current periodicals	20	17	21	21	29
Government documents	45	22	20	13	9
Company or industry data	58	16	15	11	8
Standards and specifications	0	0	0	0	1
Books or monographs not owned	0	0	1	0	3
Books on business & popular works on finance and management	0	0	0	4	2
Magazine articles not in the collection	0	0	0	0	2
Investment information sources	0	0	1	0	0
Monographs on esoteric topics in real estate	0	2	0	0	0

In 67 cases (54%), corporate libraries fill less than one percent of public library interlibrary loan requests. For 30 libraries (24%), the figures range from two to ten percent. One small city library, however, receives 25% of its materials from corporate libraries. This high figure is a result of reciprocation practices developed because of the limited number of other libraries in the area.

Twenty-six respondents (21%) indicated that they did not know the corporate library fill-rate figure, or did not answer the question. In contrast, 34 librarians (27%) were ignorant of the number of interlibrary loan requests that are fulfilled by corporate libraries.

Interlibrary loan requests from corporate libraries are not noteworthy for the majority of the responding libraries. In 44 cases (39%) the figure is less than one percent. A wider percentage range was reported by other libraries, from a low of two percent to a high of 90 percent.

In summary, the number of public libraries that use corporate libraries to fill interlibrary loan requests is not significant. It is possible to assume that corporate personnel have a greater need for public library resources than the general business community has for materials owned by large corporations. Also, the needed resources may not be unique to corporate libraries, and may be requested from academic, special, or other public libraries.

BUDGET

Forty-one (35%) of the survey respondents reported business information and reference service budget increases in the past fiscal year. One librarian specified a five percent increase, another an increase of 20%, and a third commented that the budget increased along with the inflation rate.

Funding remained the same for forty-five libraries (39%) and decreased in 30 others (26%). No money was allocated for materials from the fiscal year 1991 in a library serving a large urban area. The situation is bleak in a small city library where monies decreased in the past as well as the current fiscal years. One library's previously reduced budget is currently the same for this period. Two librarians reported increased budgets and decreased purchasing power for both the past and the present fiscal years.

One possible source of supplementary help is the large corporation wishing to express satisfaction with public library service in a tangible way. Of the 52 libraries that reported receiving benefits from corporations, 39 (75%) were given contributions, and 25 (48%) obtained books and monographs—an encouraging trend. Ten libraries (19%) receive gifts of newspaper and/or journal subscriptions, and five (10%) benefit by receiving equipment and computer systems. Service subsidies (three libraries or 6% receive these) and software (one library-1%) are not common benefits, albeit attractive ones.

Other benefits provided by corporations are described as follows:

Percentage	(number of libraries)	Benefits
8%	4	An occasional donation of money or used equipment is received
6%	3	Corporations provide speakers for programs free of charge
1%	1	The library is generally given credit in the newspaper when helping the local newspaper library

Percentage	(number of libraries)	Benefits
1%	1	Donations of business service subsidies and equipment or computer systems received from a business group, primarily made up of corporate members
1%	1	Funds for systemwide services have been solicited from businesses—for example, the online catalog
1%	1	A network of personal contacts is enlarged
1%	1	Verbal thanks and positive PR is received
1%	1	A microfilm reader and printer was given to the library
1%	1	Maps, pencils, paper and other materials are donated

Contributions from corporations influence decisions to purchase materials of great potential use in 20 libraries (39%), while corporate funding is a factor in the acquisition of resources that are of only occasional potential use in just ten libraries (19%). Twenty-two libraries (42%) that benefit from corporate contributions did not answer the question, perhaps because pencils, pens, verbal thanks, and the like have no relationship to acquisitions decisions.

EVALUATION

Collecting a variety of quantitative data is important to 89 (72%) of the 124 responding libraries. No category of data collected is the single most important criterion for service evaluation, but collection development policy assessment (42 libraries-47%) and the sources used to answer individual questions (40 libraries-45%) seem to be the most frequent queries. Analysis of interlibrary loan requests received and filled is important to 37 libraries (42%), but only nine of the respondents (10%) consider the related study of the use of networks and resource sharing as important. The easier study of interlibrary loan is more significant than measurement of the efficiency and quality of networks, document delivery and resource sharing activity.

Other methods of evaluation used are as follows:

Percentage	(number of libraries)	Data Collected
40%	36	Percent of questions answered and not answered
38%	34	Analysis of the number of questions asked and answered or not answered
36%	32	User satisfaction interview or questionnaire results
24%	21	Number of CD-ROM and online database searches run and success and accuracy rates
21%	19	Number of referrals to special libraries and types of libraries used

Thirteen libraries each listed other criteria used for evaluation:

- Collection assessment, set acquisitions goals, re-evaluation of the collection
- Circulation count, in-house usage, number of questions received
- Bi-weekly statistics on reference questions and directional questions
- Comments by the public and media
- Staff and reader suggestions
- Analysis of population served and small business information sources
- Total number of questions received
- Patron evaluation forms
- Independent study by local broker
- Number of individuals using the department daily and the nature of their telephone and in-person requests
- Polling of area businesses regarding library needs
- Patron comments and suggestions
- Output measures done annually, with business reference not separated from other reference service

Thirty-five libraries (28%) either did not answer the question or indicated that no data was collected. One librarian gave a standard reason, commenting that staff is unfortunately too busy to monitor the level of service provided. He added that emphasis is placed on "doing," without thinking about it. The level of service to businesspeople is certainly questionable if one cannot or does not step back and examine current activities in relation to the library's mission.

Just what are the differences between public library and corporate library service, as far as information and reference goals, policies and operations are concerned? The following chapter examines current practices in corporate libraries, selected from the American Library Association's directory corresponding to public libraries serving the same geographical areas.

3

Corporate Library Services: An Overview of Present Activity

In order to ascertain current levels of corporate library service provided to employees and outside users, a sample representative of various areas of the United States and of various industries was chosen for the study. A select group of libraries located in large well-known companies were included in order to obtain an overview of current activity, and to determine just how much attention is paid to the information needs of the business community outside of the corporate family.

RESPONDENTS

Of the 100 questionnaires sent directly to corporate libraries, 47 (47%) responded. Thirty-two questionnaires (63%), sent via 51 Special Libraries Association chapter presidents, were returned. As expected, the respondents serve companies in a variety of industries, including technological and computer equipment, beverages, detergents, oil, publishing, paper, investment, insurance, electronics, foods, pharmaceuticals, chemicals, automotive, photographic products, energy, communication, textiles, aeronautics, electrical, legal, engineering, metal products, and banking. These company libraries have similarities and differences that are not specific in terms of geographical location or industry type.

General Information

No organizational arrangement was found to be common to the 79 survey respondents, but 38 (48%) have corporate main libraries. Nine (11%) are satellite libraries. Just five (6%) are situated in the main library of a company that also has satellites located in other corporate offices. Another five (6%) are resource centers, and four (5%) represent one of several autonomous libraries located in corporate offices in different states. Two (3%) are division libraries. Other organizational categories are described by 16 respondents (21 as %) follows:

- One of several subject-specific collections at a single large manufacturing/corporate location—there are three main collections and six satellite libraries;
- First among equals;
- An independent division library which buys some services from a central corporate library;
- One of three which serves special needs;
- Separate corporate and law library serving the corporate headquarters and divisions; other divisions have separate technical libraries;
- Two libraries—corporate and law, with other satellite collections in such departments as tax and labor relations; a third research and development library is located in another state;
- One of four subject specific libraries—a science library;
- Serves corporate-wide business/biomedical needs;
- An independent departmental library—there is no centralized library in the company
- A library for corporate headquarters and some OPCOS (operating companies)—network with other OPCOS;
- One of two main libraries jointly managed, with other satellites informally linked; *One of twelve sites in the corporate network;
- A corporate library serving the eastern region of the United States— there is a western counterpart;
- The only library in the corporation;
- A department library not linked to the corporate library;
- The main library in a wholly owned subsidiary of a major corporation.

Corporate libraries do not tend to have staff available to provide service beyond business hours; in some cases there may not be a need to do so. Professional staff is available in the evenings for four newspaper, one textile, and three technological or computer equipment companies (10%). Saturday hours are common to the same four newspaper libraries, as well as six research and development library departments (36%). One newspaper, and three research and development library departments provide Sunday service (5%).

The method of access in three libraries (4%) that offer 24 hour service is as follows:

- The staff of an oil company library has card access to the door.
- An electronics firm's technical library is accessible at all hours but its staff is present for just nine and a half of those hours.
- No evening, Saturday, or Sunday hours are scheduled for a chemical company, but the library staff works late and on weekends and is always available to personnel.

COLLECTION

Collections must be inclusive and up-to-date to effectively meet the information needs of corporate personnel. Seventy-five of the responding libraries (95%) have the general reference titles such as dictionaries and encyclopedias. Seventy-two (91%) keep subject and industry-specific newspapers and journals, while 67 (85%) have a general newspapers and journals collection. Subject-specific indexes are common to 65 libraries (82%).

Other resources available are as follows:

Percent	(number of libraries)	Resources
78%	62	Government documents
78%	62	Specialized monographs
76%	60	Newsletters
73%	58	Industry data, statistics, trends
73%	58	Aassociation publications
72%	57	Company reports and corporate data
53%	42	Data on domestic and foreign trends and activities
53%	42	Market and consumer studies
51%	40	Doctoral dissertations and theses
43%	34	Newspaper clipping files
39%	31	Patent and trademark data
35%	28	Local and state regulations and reports
29%	23	Case histories pertaining to corporate activities and company history
29%	23	Legal indexes, dictionaries, encyclopedias
23%	18	Non-fiction titles not specific to company needs
15%	12	Company correspondence

Percent	(number of libraries)	Resources
14%	11	Collection for casual reading
11%	9	Videos, CDs, laserdiscs, audiotapes
8%	6	Technical reports, educational materials, tax forms, software, maps and atlases
8%	6	Company technical notebooks
8%	6	Conference proceedings and transactions of technical organizations
6%	5	Corporate annual reports and archives
5%	4	Law collection—case reports, statutes, regulations, treatises, practice books, court rules
5%	4	Historical photos of company operation and individual and archival materials
4%	3	Telephone directories
3%	2	Language tapes
1%	1	Cultural information, business in other countries
1%	1	Subject file of abstracted journal articles
1%	1	Historic collection
1%	1	Training videos

It is interesting to note that training videos, and other videos, compact discs, laserdiscs, and audio tapes are common to computer product, technological equipment, and a communications company library with an expected need for them. But an electronics and oil corporation also use these valuable media.

Of course, newspaper photograph collections are kept by newspaper libraries, but of interest are the historical and archival materials maintained by a detergent and an oil company.

SERVICES

About half of the libraries provide service to the general public; there is not a trend among any type of company to do so. The 37 libraries (47%) that serve outside users are associated with such industries as computer manufacture, oil, insurance, chemicals, investments, photographic products, machinery, energy, beer, textiles, technological equipment, engineering, and a law library. The level of use is quite low—ranging from less than one percent to five percent for 24 respondents (65%). Seven libraries (19%) did not give any figures because requests are too few to count. Six libraries (16%) have a higher rate of non-employee clients, as follows:

Percentage of Use	Number of Libraries	Type of Industry
95%	1	Insurance
60%	1	Energy
30%	2	Legal, textile
25%	1	Pharmaceutical
10%	1	Beer

As expected, corporate personnel have access to a full range of services, the most significant in 75 cases (95%) being ready-reference service (including photocopy) which is also the most valued for outside users in 28 of the libraries (76%) that allow access. A comparison of other services available to corporate personnel and the general public is of interest:

Percentage (number of libraries)		Type of Service
Corporate Personnel	Outside Users	
95%-75	30%-11	Retrieval of hard-to-find or obscure information
94%-74	19%- 7	Mediated online database searching
90%-71	57%-21	Telephone reference service
89%-70	19%- 7	Interlibrary loan for items not in the collection
84%-66	0%- 0	SDI service, including bibliographic data and abstracts (librarian searches)
84%-66	41%-15	Telefascimile service
73%-58	8%- 3	Editing of downloaded search results prior to delivery in printed or electronic formats
63%-50	19%- 7	End-user searching of online databases (user searches)
62%-49	16%- 6	Training programs on the use of available resources and of the collection
54%-43	0%- 0	Bibliographies of new items of interest to the corporation
47%-37	0%- 0	End-user searching training programs

Other services available to corporate users include weekly updates, CD-ROM end-user service, competitor intelligence, internal e-mail, specialized resource building, access to annual reports and printed indexes, table of contents routing, document delivery, translations, an electronic house organ, CD-ROM end-user training in personnel work areas as well as in the library, an internal network clipping service, serials routing, and consultations on information problems and library development.

It is not surprising that the 37 libraries open to the public offer a narrow range of services to outside users, but they reflect an interest in sharing resources with outsiders, as follows:

- Patrons can browse a beer company library's collection—fees are charged for copies.
- Energy and environmental kits for loan to schools are unique to an electric company library.
- The staff of an energy company library provides consultation service on library development.

Without exception, outsider access is allowed by appointment only and does not include online database searching. But a fee-based information service is being developed in a newspaper library to handle the many outside requests they receive, and service to non-competing journalists is given as a professional courtesy.

Of the 37 libraries open to the public, company records and research studies are available to non-employees in a surprising 35 cases (95%). Thirty survey respondents (81%) do not allow end-user searching. Other limitations are as follows:

Percentage	(number of libraries)	Type of limitation
49%	18	Service limited to only interlibrary loan requests and photocopies
43%	16	Service limited to requests from other librarians
27%	10	Fees charged for reference or research service
22%	8	No access or service to high school students
16%	6	Telephoned or written requests only
11%	4	Access limited to graduate students and researchers
8%	3	Access only when there is a need for specialized resources not available in other local libraries

Percentage	(number of libraries)	Type of limitations
3%	1	Searching restricted to an internal database of newspaper stories
3%	1	End-user searching limited to CD-ROM databases
3%	1	Outsiders admitted on a "space available" basis

Marketing Service

Since marketing services to corporate personnel is vital to any company library's continued existence, it was assumed that the majority (if not all survey libraries) would respond positively to the question concerning promotional media used. Sixty (76%) of the seventy-nine responding libraries do so, while 19 (24%) did not indicate whether or not they promote service, or at least appreciate the importance of such an activity. The most significant promotional media used to attract corporate users are lists of new acquisitions, a library newsletter, subject bibliographies, bookmarks, flyers or posters, and bibliographies with abstracts on new data or research. Just eight (10%) use direct mail campaigns and internal newspaper ads or articles.

Other promotional methods used to attract coporate personnel are valuable, particularly when combined with others. These include the following:

- A brochure included in new employee orientations
- Presentations to managers or through personal contact—library service is the best marketing tool
- E-mail letter with follow-up
- Promotion by information consultant
- Presentations, brochures, special services, and SDI's
- A newsletter abstracting journal articles of interest
- Presentations to other departments and at lab meetings
- Database marketing by a third party
- Regular competitive publications
- Visits to corporate departments
- Special "open house" events
- "Bag lunch" seminars
- A video on services and resources
- An E-mail newswire
- A list of library periodicals and reference sources

The assumption that services would generally not be marketed to outside users was upheld—only four libraries (5%), located in textile, technology, energy, and newspaper firms do so.

Subject bibliographies are used to promote service in the textile company library, while the technology company uses bookmarks, flyers, posters, and a special fee-based research service for outside users. The newspaper library shows evidence of more activity in attracting outsiders by distributing a newsletter, holding exhibits at business and industry fairs and conventions, and making available a special fee-based search service. The energy firm's librarian listed a surprising variety of promotional media—newspaper ads and articles, bookmarks, flyers, posters, exhibits at business and industry fairs and conventions, subject bibliographies, lists of new acquisitions, bibliographies with abstracts on new data and research, direct mail campaigns, a special fee-based research service, and visits to public libraries. This company clearly has a commitment to serving the business community's information needs.

COOPERATION AND PUBLIC LIBRARIES

Cooperative links are obviously important to corporate libraries to ensure access to resources and information necessary for the corporation's health and profit. It is not surprising to find that cooperation with other corporate libraries is the choice for 71 (90%) of the 79 respondents, but these partnerships are likely to be within the parent company and its subsidiaries. Sixty-nine (87%) of the respondents link with college and university libraries because they hold large research collections and are often supported by corporate personnel who are alumni. Public libraries are significant partners for 66 (84%) of the survey respondents. Cooperative links with association libraries exist in 58 (73%). Other cooperative arrangements include the following:

- Any other library via telephone, fax, OCLC, ALA request;
- Public and private law libraries;
- School libraries;
- Libraries with membership in the state network;
- Other libraries within the corporation;
- Government libraries and organizations;
- Medical libraries;
- Other OCLC member libraries;
- An adopted high school library;
- Related industry libraries via a specific association.

The reasons 13 survey respondents (16%) have for not forming partnerships with any other libraries are as follows:

- There is not enough staff or time to serve outsiders and company personnel.
- The collection is too specialized to be of interest to outsiders.
- Due to the confidential scope of the collection, it is off limits to outsiders.
- The library is a very small operation with no permanent staff and can only serve the local research and development group of the company.
- There is very little public contact since any company information has to be requested from the corporate communications department.
- The local public library has very good personal investment resources; nevertheless no resource sharing arrangement has been developed.

Corporate personnel are made aware of public libraries in 54 cases (68%), but for the most part the information retrieval process is handled by the librarian. The comments of five respondents are of interest:

- They are made aware if necessary, but the need is rare.
- As a general rule, they are not.
- Announcements are placed in the newsletter, and personnel are only referred occasionally.
- What we do, not where we get it from, is stressed.
- Personnel is "blind" to where we get material.

But when the need arises 69 (87%) of the total universe of 79 corporate libraries refer corporate personnel to public libraries, using the following procedures:

Percent	(number of libraries)	Procedure
83%	57	Corporate librarian obtains information from the public library and delivers it to the patron
75%	52	Name, location and library hours given
30%	21	Corporate librarian calls public librarian to explain the request
26%	18	Corporate librarian calls public library to arrange for patron visit

Some comments regarding referral practices highlight the tendency toward exclusivity, i.e., the corporate library seems to be inadequate only when the needed information is not directly related to corporate goals. The following comments illustrate this finding:

- Clients are referred for personal research/non-business use.
- Employees are rarely referred—we usually do it for them, but the action taken depends on the nature of the request.
- Clients are referred when the request is not work-related.
- We do not refer to public libraries because we have an agreement with the local university library.
- We refer for personal or school research on topics not covered by the collection.
- No direct referrals are made but we make some use of public libraries.
- Direct referrals are given with trepidation; special library service is much better than public library service.
- We do whatever makes the customer most comfortable.
- Dial access to the public library's OPAC is provided.
- A description of the material and how it meets the client's need is provided.

Cooperation with public libraries commands special attention, and respondents provided clear-cut data on the nature of their cooperative relationship, as seen in the following table:

Table of Frequency of Requests for Resources from Public Libraries by Corporate Libraries

Ranking: Least 1   2   3   4   5 Most

Resources	Number of Libraries				
	1	2	3	4	5
Books/monographs related to individual requests not available in the corporate library	13	9	9	14	29
Articles from journals not available in the corporate library	19	3	3	16	33
Data on particular corporations	57	4	5	3	5
Information on research findings in a particular industry or corporation	58	9	3	2	2
Medical, legal, technical research data	55	5	8	2	1
Special indexes, bibliographies, dictionaries	45	7	11	3	7
Government documents, reports	33	4	16	15	6

Continued

Resources	Number of Libraries				
	1	2	3	4	5
Online databases not available in the corporate library or not searched	68	1	1	3	1
CD-ROM databases not available in the corporate library	59	1	8	2	4
General reference not in the collection	0	0	0	0	1
Occasional reference questions beyond the normal sphere, for example, color photographs of places (landmarks)needed for presentations	0	0	0	0	1
Cost of living data, university	0	0	0	0	1
Patents	0	0	0	0	1
Information for school projects, subjects out of the realm of the collection needed for work	0	0	1	0	0
Information for children's book reports, homework, etc.	0	0	1	0	0
Local materials/vertical file materials	0	0	1	0	0

Journal articles not available in corporate libraries are, similar to public library requests from corporate partners, the most requested materials. There is a trend toward reciprocal activity when it comes to filling requests for periodical articles. The same tendency holds true to a lesser degree for books and monographs related to individual requests and not available in the corporate library. Electronic resources such as online and CD-ROM databases are among the least frequently requested resources.

Only 11 survey respondents (14%) reported that public libraries impose service limitations on personnel referred to them. These include the following:

- Material is not circulated directly to the customers unless they have their own library cards and are city, county, or district residents.
- A non-resident may purchase a borrower's card.
- There is a charge for photocopying.
- Persons must have their own library card, but all in-library use is free.
- Fees are charged for online searching and interlibrary loans.

Comments on the question of referrals represent major reasons for not doing so:

"Referrals are made with trepidation because many of the staff of the closest public library need an attitude adjustment. An attitude of service and helpfulness does not characterize the business department staff."

"Patrons are not referred to public libraries because we are supposed to get what is needed, not to point someone somwhere else."

Partnerships with public libraries are not widely cultivated to add value to library service to cooperate personnel. Cooperation has increased in the past two fiscal years in 25 (32%) of the 79 corporate libraries surveyed, primarily because of the need for reference resources not available in the corporate library (60%-15 libraries.) Five of these respondents (20%) indicated that greater cooperation was caused by an inadequate budget and the rising cost of materials, the development of a public library business information service that fills information needs rapidly and thoroughly, and a greater demand for a variety of journals located via online databases. Membership in cooperative networks and the expected resource sharing and reciprocation increased partnerships in eight libraries (32%).

A newspaper company library indicated that corporate library listings in directories caused an increase in cooperation, while an electronics firm librarian noted that a book that lists the periodicals held in all cooperating libraries, published by a regional system, caused increased activity in this area. Workloads and a greater variety of work in a communications library resulted in the establishment of greater cooperative links with public libraries.

Although the sample is small, the responses seem to point to a growing tendency toward less corporate library isolation, and greater recognition of the importance of cooperation for resource sharing, information retrieval, and document delivery.

ELECTRONIC SERVICES

The significnce of databases for increasing efficiency and retrieving information that is more up-to-date than print materials is recognized by the surveyed libraries. The 50 respondents (63%) who provide end-user searching, as well as the nine (11%) who do not allow that practice, tend to acquire a wide variety of CD-ROM databases. Some of the surveyed libraries have so many different products that they listed them only by subject—for example, newspapers, technical data, tax, patents.

  ABI/INFORM is the most widely used CD-ROM product—followed by *Compact Disclosure*. Of the databases used by a only a few libraries, no significant pattern by type of industry was evident. For example, *Business Abstracts* is available in an electronics, cereal, and chemical company business library; *Standard & Poors Corporations* is available in two electronics, two chemical, and a computer company. The same computer company, plus two oil firms, an aeronautics, photographic products, and an electronics company have *Thomas Register*.

  The number of CD-ROM databases available in two or more corporate libraries is impressive, as the following table illustrates:

Percentage	(number of libraries)	CD-ROM Databases
69%	24	*ABI/INFORM*
22%	13	*Compact Disclosure*
17%	10	*Computer Select*
10%	6	*Thomas Register*
10%	6	*BIP Plus*
8%	5	*Standard & Poor's Corporations*
8%	5	*Moody's*
7%	4	*Business Abstracts*
7%	4	*National Trade Databank*
5%	3	*Business Dateline*
5%	3	*Medline*
5%	3	*SEC Online (Silver Platter)*
5%	3	*IEEE/IEE on Disc*
5%	2	*Computer Database*
3%	2	*U.S. Trade (Imports-Exports)*
3%	2	*Inspec*
3%	2	*Dun's Business Locator*

  Other CD-ROM databases which corporate libraries access include:

- *DDA Phone America*
- *Avaition Compendium*
- *Compton's Encyclopedia*
- *Metatex*
- *Compendex Plus*
- *MicroPatent Patent Databases*
- *World Weather Disc*
- *McGraw Hill Science & Technology Reference Set*
- *Agricola*
- *Wilsondisc*
- *U.S. Census*

- *NewsBank*
- *EBSCO's Magazine Article Summaries*
- *Worldwide Standards Index*
- *Polytax I/II*
- *InfoTrac Business Collection*
- *CIA World Factbook*
- *SCITECH Reference Plus*
- *Food Science & Technology Abstracts*
- *Official Gazette and Patent Office*
- *U.S. Patent Images (from Rapid Patent International)*
- *Patentview*
- *International Pharmaceutical Abstracts*
- *Drug Information Source*
- *Cancerlit*
- *Microsoft Bookshelf*
- *Wall Street Journal On-disc*
- *OG/Plus, Food Analyst*
- *Gale Global Associations*
- *Federal Register*
- *Granger's*
- *LC MARC*
- *A.M. Best*
- *Martindale Hubbell*

Access to data on CD-ROM is extended in a cost-saving way by a computer company. Its east coast library has access to Compact Disclosure and Thomas Register via a LAN (Local Area Network) linked to a remote site in a western state.

It is no surprise that more corporate libraries have access to online databases than those on CD-ROM because the information available is more current, and frequently updated in 24 hours or less. Seventy-six libraries (96%) use more than one vendor system, with some reporting subscriptions to more than ten. *DIALOG* is the system of choice for 74 corporate libraries (94%). Presumably the newspaper library that has the now defunct *VU/TEXT* either picked up *DIALOG*, where most of the full-text newspaper files became available, or searches them via *CompuServe*—another system mentioned. Thirty-four other *VU/TEXT* subscribers (46%) also have access to *DIALOG*. A pharmaceutical company is currently without the *VU/TEXT* files, but searches *DataStar*.

Fifty-two libraries (66%) subscribe to *NEXIS*, 46 (58%) access *Dow Jones News Retrieval*, and 29 (37%) search *ORBIT*. *NewsNet, Wilsonline*, and *BRS* are available in 20 libraries (25%). Other systems searched include the folowing:

Percentage	(number of libraries)	Online Systems
23%	18	*STN*
16%	13	*DataStar*
16%	13	*DataTimes*
9%	7	*NLM Medline*
9%	7	*Dun's Direct Access*
8%	6	*Reuters*
8%	6	*EPIC (OCLC)*
5%	4	*LEXIS*
5%	4	*PIERS*
4%	3	*Investext (direct access)*
4%	3	*HRIN*
4%	3	*Questel*
3%	2	*Paperchase*
3%	2	*InfoGlobe*
3%	2	*Westlaw*
3%	2	*CompuServe*
3%	2	*Textline*
1%	1	*Washington Alert*
1%	1	*Foodline*
1%	1	*Oil & Gas Journal*
1%	1	*Pergamon*
1%	1	*Aviation/Aerospace Online*

For 62 survey libraries (78%) these systems are used to search only databases that are specific to the corporation's needs. Eight respondents (10%) that search online for other than corporate-specific information charge fees to employees.

Topping the list of are *ABI/INFORM* (56%-44 libraries), *PTS Prompt* (54%-43 libraries), and *Trade & Industry Index* (47%-37 libraries.) Many other databases were mentioned by at least one library and as many as 30. They include the following:

Percentage	(number of libraries)	Database
37%	29	*Investext*
34%	27	*D&B Dun's Financial Records*
27%	21	*Standard & Poors News*
25%	20	*Management Contents*
23%	18	*Business Dateline*
23%	18	*Trademarkscan*
23%	18	*Disclosure Spectrum/Ownership*
22%	17	*D&B Donnelly Demographics*

Continued

Percentage	(number of libraries)	Database
13%	10	*Chemical Industry Notes*
13%	10	*NTIS*
11%	9	*Compendex*
10%	8	*Business Software Database*
10%	8	*CENDATA*
10%	8	*Health Planning & Administration*
10%	8	*Inspec*
9%	7	*Business Periodicals Index*
8%	6	*American Banker Full Text*
8%	6	*PAIS International*
8%	6	*Chemical Abstracts*
6%	5	*Pharmaceutical News Index*
6%	5	*Patents*
5%	4	*BioBusiness*
5%	4	*Computer Database*
5%	4	*Foods Adlibra*
5%	4	*Medline*
4%	3	*Metatex*
3%	2	*World Patents*
1%	1	*Labordoc*
1%	1	*Energyline/Environline*
1%	1	*Dow Jones News*
1%	1	*Chemical Business Newsbase*
1%	1	*GEOREF*

A number of respondents use many databases so frequently they identified them only by subject,—for example, technical, scientific, full-text newspapers, statistical.

Twenty-seven libraries (34%) limit online searching for corporate personnel by charging fees. Restrictions such as the number of databases searched, the number of citations printed, the number of abstracts with citations printed, the number of full text records printed, and the time spent on the search are insignificant because they apply to only one percent to four percent of the surveyed libraries.

Other restrictions mentioned are tied to charges, cost, and the budget as follows:

- Some costs are backcharged to the department.
- A combination of all the limitations listed on the questionnaire is balanced against the need for the information—there is no cut and dry policy.
- The client is charged if there is an unreasonably large amount of time and hits involved.

- Fees are charged to non-research and development personnel; there is a charge for very extensive searches over $50.00.
- There is a charge if the cost is over $250.00 online.
- There are no limitations on legitimate business requests, although the librarian determines what budget the person feels is appropriate for the project and then stays within that budget.
- There are no rules since it is a judgement call by the information professional involved.

Corporate library fee policies are not quite as varied or daunting as those of public libraries, but efforts to control costs while increasing efficiency are equally problematic. Charging practices for corporate personnel were defined by the survey respondents as follows:

- This depends on final use—internal use charge and invoiced client engagements: invoice x 2.
- If the search is less than $200, cost is charged back to user's department.
- Primary clients are free; others are back-charged unless the cost is minimal; special projects are back-charged if they have funds.
- Direct costs for personnel.
- Corporate personnel are charged a flat fee per search, plus online searches if they exceed $250.
- Costs of the actual search are charged back to the client's division.
- Search charges are charged back to corporate users through budget codes; there is no charge for staff time.
- Search costs for searches $85and over are charged back to corporate personnel.
- The cost of searching is covered in the annual budget and not charged back under ordinary circumstances. External information brokers' search charges are not charged back to our customers.
- Corporate personnel are charged $45 an hour for research; also charge by the half hour; less than this, there is no charge.
- We do whatever they will pay for.
- The price of the search is charged to other departments.
- Departments that contribute to the library allocation are not charged; non-allocation users are charged staff time and database costs (connect time and prints).
- It is department specific—out-of-pocket fees only are charged—no charge for staff time.
- We charge our people on-site actual costs for searches that are more than "quickies"; others from the company (those outside our site) are charged actual cost plus $60 labor.
- There is no charge for searches under $15; over $15 is charged to a valid corporate charge number.

- Currently charge if over $250 online cost. In 1993 we will charge for search and search time.
- Outside of the department, charged back for complete search per database—staff time is not included.
- Charge only when monthly budget is exceeded.
- Over $50.00 in connect time charges are back-billed; there is no charge for research and development staff.
- Charged for online time, print charges and searcher's time.
- $25 search charge; 13% surcharge; cost for online time and citations.
- In 1992, online costs plus time at $75 an hour x 2; in 1993, charge-back will cease and all will return to overhead charges.
- Charged cost of the search and a fee for anything over and including $200.

As expected, corporate libraries do not encourage ouside use of the wealth of systems and databases they access, since disemmination of information within the corporation is a priority. But there are exceptions. Online database searching is available to outside users in seven of the responding libraries (9%)—a financial firm, an oil company, the technical library of an aeronautics corporation, a textile manufacturer, an engineering company, a chemical firm and an energy corporation.

The databases most frequently searched for outsiders are as follows:

Industry	Databases
Textile	*ABI/INFORM*
Financial	*CENDATA*
Chemical	*Chemical Industry Notes*
Oil	*Standard & Poors News*
	Trademarkscan
Energy	*Health Planning and Administration*
	Trade & Industry Index
Engineering	*Inspec*
	Compendex
Aeronautics	*PTS Prompt*

The practice of charging outsiders for online searching is not surprising. The general public tends to expect to pay for access to databases, particularly in special libraries in the for-profit sector. The energy corporation imposes charges as well as two other limitations—the number of citations printed and the time spent on the search.

The engineering company charges a higher fee than for corporate personnel. Online searching costs the outsider $75 per hour for the librarian's time, plus online charges, at the aeronautics company. Outside users are charged if the search is not directly related to the energy corporation's product.

Nine survey libraries (11%) waive limitations for outside users willing to pay full cost, including staff time. The reasons for not lifting restrictions are insufficient staff and time, and the fact that database contracts do not allow online searching for non-employees. An oil company librarian stated that limitations may be waived in the future, but the reason for this change was not given.

NETWORKS AND INTERLIBRARY LOAN

The practice of participating in networks for the purpose of supplementing collections and obtaining needed information from other libraries via electronic mail or fax is significant to 60 survey libraries (76%). Of the 60, 42 (70%) belong to OCLC, and 25 (42%) are members of regional library networks. Because a high percentage of public libraries also belong to these networks, one might assume that public libraries have experienced increased requests for information from their corporate counterparts. Other networks include the following:

Percentage	(number of libraries)	Network
20%	12	Corporate network
12%	7	Metropolitan area network
10%	6	RLIN
8%	5	ILLINET
5%	3	WLN
3%	2	NELINET
2%	1	Michigan Library Consortium
2%	1	CLASS

Interlibrary loan use is obviously important to ensure access to the resources and information needed by the corporate community. The respondents supplied information on the nature of their interlibrary loan use, as seen in the following table:

Significance of Resources to Corporate
Library Interlibrary Loan Use

Ranking: Least 1 2 3 4 5 Most

Resources	Number of Libraries				
	1	2	3	4	5
Resources in other subject fields	22	9	10	18	16
Obscure, scholarly periodicals	28	11	8	12	16
Dissertations, theses	42	12	10	8	5
Non-current periodicals	18	2	14	17	24
General newspapers, journals	32	7	11	15	10
Government documents	35	5	14	12	9
Other corporate or industry data	48	4	11	3	9
Out-of-print books	0	0	0	0	1
Materials not owned in the company library	0	0	0	0	1
Out-of-print technical monographs	0	0	0	0	1
Patents	0	0	0	0	1
Periodicals missing from the collection	0	0	1	0	1
Books on business and popular works on finance and management	0	1	1	0	2

A computer company librarian commented that their clients have a broad base of interests; although they subscribe to over 800 periodicals, they still rely heavily on interlibrary loan because of these broad interests. Public libraries are probably relied upon because their collections are more inclusive. Further evidence of this need can be seen in the materials obtained most often from public libraries:

Percentage	(number of libraries)	Materials
35%	28	Newspapers and magazines not held in the collection
29%	23	Resources in subject fields outside the main interests
24%	19	General non-fiction, technical, out-of-print books
9%	7	General reference material
5%	4	Government documents
3%	2	Articles not available online in full-text

Percentage	(number of libraries)	Materials
1%	1	Statistics, photographs
1%	1	Company, marketing data
1%	1	Local history
1%	1	Books on resumes, management topics
1%	1	Arts and humanities
1%	1	Patent material

The number of interlibrary loan requests received is interesting. Thirty respondents (38%) did not provide figures. The extent to which the entire universe of 79 corporate libraries uses public libraries to fill interlibrary loan requests cannot be accurately measured because of this missing data, but low use is suggested by the available information. Twelve libraries (15%) indicated that only one percent or less of their interlibrary loan requests are filled by public libraries, but another 12 (15%) reported a fill rate ranging from 20-25%. Seven libraries (9%) obtain two to three percent of their borrowed materials from public libraries, and 11 (14%) listed a range from five to 15 percent. Surprisingly, seven (9%) obtain 50-100% of the materials not in their collections from public libraries. The libraries reporting the highest fill rates are located in two newspaper companies, a communications firm and a financial corporation.

A newspaper library rarely uses interlibrary loan because it takes too long. Even though 95 percent of their requests are filled by public libraries, either a document delivery service is used or the staff goes to the public library to obtain the needed materials. In addition, a financial company almost never uses public libraries because they are too understaffed to be time-responsive.

Public library interlibrary loan requests for materials owned by corporate libraries respondents are usually for unique resources or information that cannot otherwise be obtained. These include the following:

Percentage	(number of libraries)	Materials
43%	34	Books or journal articles that are subject-specific to the corporation's mission or products
14%	11	Technical information
9%	7	Company information
3%	2	Government documents
1%	1	Books that are on OCLC
1%	1	Career data (e.g., resume writing for scientists and engineers
1%	1	Environmental information
1%	1	Legislative material

Twenty-eight corporate libraries (35%) receive less than one percent of their interlibrary loan requests from public libraries. In ten cases (1%)], the figure is three to five percent. The figures for the remaining survey respondents range widely from ten percent to as high as 95 percent. The highest rate of interlibrary loans requested by public libraries are received by a newspaper library (95%), a technical equipment company (80%), and an oil company (75%).

Some corporate libraries do not loan their materials to anyone other than their own employees because of the proprietary nature of the collection, as well as the primary function of the library—collection and dissemination of information for the corporate benefit.

BUDGET

Corporate downsizing has had a profound effect on the health and continued existence of company libraries. Of the total universe of 79 libraries, the majority experienced budget increases in a two-year period. Thirty-nine (49%) reported a budget increase in the first fiscal year, but the figure decreased to 43% (34) in the second.

Twenty-one (27%) kept the same budget in the first fiscal year, but just 17 respondents (22%) held on to the same amount of funding in the next year.

Allocations went down in just 14 libraries (18%) one year, but the budgets of 23 libraries (29%) decreased in the next fiscal year. Five of the survey respondents (6%) did not provide any budgetary information.

In the light of the negative economic trend, it is not surprising that just 21 of the survey library corporations (27%) compensate public libraries as a result of satisfaction with their services—tight budgets limit generosity. One financial corporation librarian reacted to the idea of giving to public libraries with an emphatic negative, since they pay a "stiff local tax."

How public libraries are compensated is of interest. The means of compensation are as follows:

Percentage	(number of libraries)	Compensation
57%	12	Funding and contributions
14%	3	Books and monographs
10%	2	Service subsidies
10%	2	Volunteer work
10%	2	Taxes and specific fees for services
5%	1	Previous year's reference books
5%	1	Equipment and computer systems
5%	1	Buy $100 a year business service card

The importance of a company's partnership with public libraries can be partially determined by the availability of certain corporate library services and resources and the need to duplicate them. Forty of the survey respondents (51%) do consider what the public library has to offer to be significant—a surprising response when considering the low interlibrary loan figures.

EVALUATION

Corporate libraries must prove that they are essential to the corporation by providing quality service and information to improve decision making, company productivity, and profits. Without formal evaluation, corporate libraries have difficulty proving value and justifying their continued existence. No common method of measurement is used by the responding libraries. The data collected include the following:

Percentage	(number of libraries)	Data collected
70%	46	User satisfaction, interview, or questionnaire results
39%	26	Analysis of interlibrary loan requests and requests filled
36%	24	Number of CD-ROM, online database searches run and success rate/rate of accuracy
32%	21	Analysis of the number of questions asked, answered, not answered
29%	19	Sources used to answer individual questions
29%	19	Assessment of collection development policy and procedure
24%	16	Percent of questions answered, not answered
11%	7	Results of study of use of networks and resource sharing
11%	7	Number of referrals to other libraries and types of libraries used

An assortment of different data elements are collected by some of the survey libraries. These include the following:

• Simple statistics, such as the number of interlibrary loan and photocopy requests, the number of items ordered for customers and the collection, the number of items circulated, the number of SDIs and consultations, the number of online vendor invoices processed and passwords requested. Customer satisfaction on major information resource projects is also measured;

- Statistics on loaned materials, reference requests, articles sent, tables of contents sent, Three surveys were conducted in nine years;
- Flowtimes for service and delivery throughout libraries are tracked;
- General customer satisfaction is measured, response time and fill rates are analyzed, and staff satisfaction with the completeness of answers and satisfaction with systems is studied;
- An annual customer satisfaction survey is conducted;
- Letters of response are used as an indication of support for library service,and the percentage of increase of the annual output is analyzed;
- Evaluation is conducted by a library advisory committee;
- Project-accounting data is analyzed, as is executive feedback, the use statistics, number of calls, number of books circulated, and so forth.

Thirteen responding libraries (16%) do not collect data and have no means of formally justifying their continued existence. Comments suggest that corporate economic difficulties are or will result in the harsh reality of extinction as follows:

"We are a 'seat of the pants' and 'do what works' operation with temporary staff."

"We do not evaluate. Our library is being downscaled drastically."

"We have no time to collect data."

In any library the level of service, as well as the continued health and vitality of corporate libraries depends on the quality and quantity of evaluatory procedures. Clearly, the operational constraints that result in service deficiencies must be carefully and thoroughly examined.

4

A Service Alternative: The Academic Library

Fee-based services in academic libraries allow reference, information retrieval, and document delivery to be extended to business clientele who are not being adequately served in some geographical areas, perhaps due to small public library systems, inadequate public library business collections, a limited number of special libraries, or no local information brokers. Although academic libraries house the most substantial research collection in many locations throughout the United States, they do not have the staff or funding to provide needed information as rapidly as is often required by members of the business community. A fee-based service is viewed as a way of enhancing academic library service to meet the demands of those in the private sector who are knocking on university and college doors without taking any staff and funds away from service to the primary clientele—the faculty and students.

The reasons for establishing this type of service in an academic environment, where it might seem at odds with the library's mission, are quite varied. Often, it just grew because the business community recognized the university library as the best source for a valuable commodity for which it was quite willing to pay—information. Frequent requests from corporate personnel, entrepreneurs, and small business owners and staff for access to the available services and resources, including borrowing privileges, resulted in an examination of the possibilities for accommodating them.

In other cases, academia wanted to establish closer ties with local business and industry to increase awareness of, and involvement in university programs and activities which would ultimately benefit collection and curriculum development, particularly for the business school. Contributing to the excellence and quality of the graduates would ultimately serve the best interests of individual companies, and the economy as a whole.

Other reasons for developing fee-based services include the following:

• The private sector has a right to access in state or city universities, because they are supported by taxpayer monies;
• The academic library is the only library in the area to offer access to online information retrieval;
• Such a service would attract businesspersons who are alumni with money to support the alma mater;
• Providing access to small businesses (and large corporations) that cannot afford their own libraries is good for public relations—a "friend" in the community helping to achieve economic success;
• The academic library is a member of a cooperative network, and with access to its resources are expected;
• The services and resources available are included in library directory listings;
• Charging fees to outsiders is a way of recovering costs, as well as generating additional funding for the expense of operation, staff time, equipment, and the use of other departments (e.g., interlibrary loan).

In order to obtain a snapshot view of the similarities and differences among academic libraries that provide fee-based services, a questionnaire was sent to twenty-five colleges and universities, selected from the *FISCAL Directory of Fee-Based Information Services in Libraries*. Seventeen responses were received from the managers of such services located in Colorado, District of Columbia, Florida (2 libraries), Georgia, Illinois, Louisiana, New Jersey, New York (3 libraries), Oregon, South Carolina, Texas (3 libraries), and Utah.

Of the respondents that serve the local business community, eleven provide statewide access as well, and nine also allow use by clientele located out-of-state.

Corporate personnel and corporate library staff are the most frequest users in the majority of the responding libraries, while the personnel of small- and medium-sized businesses, entrepreneurs and self-employed, researchers, technicians, and students from other colleges and universities are less numerous. Government officials and job seekers tend to be moderate users. (Perhaps because they either have access elsewhere, have no need for frequent use, or cannot afford the fees on a regular basis.) Use by public library staff is insignificant, allowing the inference that their business collections are adequate for their patrons, or that they are unaware of what is available in the academic library.

One respondent indicated heavy use by fee-based information brokerage services, as well as by university faculty doing personal research. In another case, use by personnel of large corporations was emphasized. Surprisingly, students from area high schools are frequent users in a southern state university.

The information brokering services established in academic libraries often do not include full access to all services and resources, however high the demand may be. The collections and staff size are frequently not large enough to adequately and efficiently serve the needs of students and faculty as well as the needs of members of the business community, who have high expectations for rapid and all-inclusive service. The strength of fee-based, on-demand service lies in the retrieval of accurate, current information for immediate business decisions that is delivered with the requisite speed.

For corporations which need data that is outside of the scope of their own library resources, the academic library's fee-based service is value-added, and well worth the expense. Although it may be an attractive information retrieval and delivery option for large and small companies without their own libraries, entrepreneurs, and others in need of business-related information, the cost may be problematic.

The responses received by the 17 librarians who answered the questionnaire serve to illustrate just how broad or narrow fee-based services can be. The collections and services provided, as well as the limitations, fees, and request and payment policies are briefly described as follows:

1. Mediated searching is done on DIALOG, BRS, and STN at $125 per hour; end-users may retrieve information via BRS After Dark, and the Knowledge Index. The library does not charge for manual searching, but a list of searchers, who have their own fee schedules, is distributed. Photocopies are five cents per page. No fax service or book loans are available to business clients.

2. Those who come in to the library can use everything including the book collections, CD-ROMs, etc. Others can request literature searches and document delivery through the fee-based information service. This northeastern state university allows book loans to local residents who have a state driver's license. The charge for manual and online searching is $110 per hour, plus online database costs. Photocopy service is $32 per hour plus ten cents per page, while fax charges are $8 for thirty pages, and the photocopy charges. There is a fee for document delivery via express mail. Policy states that the request must have relevance to some area of industrial and labor relations. The client is billed after service is provided, except for corporate sponsors who have given donations to the school.

3. The reference works and collections of two campus libraries are available to subscribers for $50 a year. Manual and computer searches, and document delivery from the collections and outside sources are available. Use of the libraries and in-person borrowing is limited to corporate members, except for state and United States depository collections. Others are charged a fee. Manual and online searching costs $35 an hour, plus the database costs and a service charge for more complex searches. The minimum charge for manual searches is $15. The charge for photocopies is $5, plus twenty-five cents per page, and a copyright fee; fax service is $5. Book loans from library collections are $10; if from other sources, the price is $15. The patrons are billed, with reminders sent after several months. Large bills that are more than eight months overdue are sent to a collection agency.

4. Research and fact finding services are provided, including literature searches, statistics, competitor profiles, and demographics; document retrieval is significant for photocopies of journals or newspaper articles, government documents, research reports, patents, book and dissertation loans; rush service is available for an additional fee; orders are accepted in person, or by phone, fax, and mail. Manual and online searching costs $75 per hour, plus the direct costs of database fees, photocopy charges, and long-distance telephone calls. There is a one hour minimum charge. Manual ready-reference or verification services cost $18.75 if they take up to fifteen minutes to answer, or if they verify incomplete citations. Photocopies are $15 for the first 15 pages and $.25 for each additional page from the university library; the fee is $20 for the first 15 pages and $.25 for each additional page for documents from area libraries; for documents provided by other libraries, the charge is $15 per document, plus the supplier's cost. There is a $2.00 flat rate for local fax service; long distance domestic fax is $.50 per page, while international fax is at cost. A three week book loan from the university library is $15; the fee is the same for books from outside libraries, but with the supplier's cost added on; renewals are $15 per title. Referrals are $8 per title for the location of libraries that may have an item that is not available in the university library; for rush service there is a 100 percent surcharge for document requests filled within three hours; there is a $25 per hour surcharge for rush research. Document delivery is at cost for bicycle courier, car courier or overnight express; first class mail is $1.00 per letter-size package, and $3.00 for book-size package, while international mail is at cost for postage. Requests are taken for documents and research by telephone, fax, mail or in-person, but for complex projects an appoint-

ment with the researcher is recommended. If more that two documents are requested, the client is asked to either fax or mail the request, noting when the material is needed, the desired means of delivery, and any client or project number to be included on the invoice. A monthly invoice, with a summary of activity and services, is sent to the client. Payment is due on receipt of the invoice and can be made by check, VISA or MasterCard.

5. An extensive collection on a variety of subjects is available for literature searches, for example, bibliographies, numeric data, directory information; reports/summaries of literature searches are prepared; current awareness (SDI) is provided to keep up to date on topics of interest; document delivery includes copies of journal articles, patents, standards, specifications and technical reports. No in-person book loans are allowed, but they are available via interlibrary loan if the company has a library, an information center, or an information officer to be responsible as an intermediary. Manual and online searching is $75 an hour, plus database, photocopy, and delivery charges.

   Rush service is $125 and hour, plus a $10 surcharge per item for 24 hour dispatch; additional charges are applied for overnight delivery and postal rates. There is a $15 flat fee for photocopies for up to ten pages from paper or fiche; it is $.25 per page for over ten pages, and $2.00 per fiche for over two fiche. Fax costs $1.00 per page for the United States, and $2.00 per page outside the United States. Book loans are $15 per item, with regular service limited to agencies with a library or information officer. Requests are accepted by mail, fax,telephone, and OCLC; payment is by monthly invoice, VISA or MasterCard—deposit accounts are available for customer convenience.

6. This small college's community information service offers such services as reference and research service, online database searching, interlibrary loan, borrowing privileges and document delivery. *Standard & Poors Executives & Corporations,* and *Valuline* are available. The respondent commented that the director decided that *Dun & Bradstreet's Million Dollar Directory* was unnecessary; *Business Newsbank* was also discontinued. The librarian also stated that the business section is very inadequate. Online searching costs involve only the database and searching charges that must be paid at the time of the search—there is no surcharge. No limitations were given for manual searching.

7. Service to members includes such resources as Moody's, Standard & Poor's, and Dun & Bradstreet directories, as well as reports, guides, periodicals, and more housed in a standard business library collection, plus a very comprehensive collection of retrospective

directories, annual reports and 10Ks; there is access to online services plus CD-ROM products for those who are members. If clients are not a member of the business resource center they have no borrowing privileges, no access to online searching, and cannot use the library during restricted periods of the semester. Online searching charges include the basic online cost plus a 15 percent surcharge, while manual research costs from $40 to $70 per research hour. Photocopies are $10 to $15 per article; fax is $10 plus $1 per page; $15 per book is charged for book loans. There is a membership advantage for requests and payments; new clients may open a deposit account for $250. At present, no credit cards are accepted.

8. This western state university has a fine collection of 1.3 million volumes, with strengths in such areas as engineering, agriculture, forestry, aquaculture, oceanography, and applied sciences that is accessible for in-house use or via a borrowers card; other services are interlibrary loan, online searching, CD-ROM databases, reference service, and document delivery. Online searching is done by appointment only (cost recovery plus $20) for all clients. If an outsider is not a local resident, a borrower's card is available via Friends of the Library membership. Photocopies are ten cents per page, and fax service costs $7.50 per minute and $.75 per page. This state library does not yet have a request/payment policy. They are in the process of developing a complete fee-for-service package (perhaps by subscription) for the non-university community, including businesses.

9. Business and science collections are used by the business community. The library, open to anyone, is adequate to support masters programs in business and engineering. Some services to local organizations that pay an annual membership fee of $40 are provided, including photocopies, free book loans, interlibrary loan ($6), and online database searching (cost plus $8). Research services are not available. Photocopies cost $3 if under ten pages; if over ten pages the charge is $2 plus ten cents per page. Fax service has a $1.50 charge attached to it. If someone is not affiliated with the university, they must pay fees for services in advance; if an organization has paid for library membership, they are billed at the end of the month.

10. The collection includes eight million volumes with 38,000 periodical subscriptions in all disciplines, plus research reports, directories, mailing lists, company profiles; statistical tracking of a number of documents published in topic areas over time, bibliographies, and statistics are available. Services include document delivery, fact finding (quick search for facts), online database searching, current

awareness, competitor intelligence, library research, indexing and abstracting, and translations. The service was begun to accommodate non-university affiliated persons for a fee, which includes all services available to regular patrons. Manual and online searching charges are variable, and involve an additional $60 charge plus costs (one hour minimum) for research. Photocopies are ten cents per page, while fax service costs $2 per page. Books loaned from the university library are $15; from other sources the charge is $15 plus the supplier's cost. Faculty consultation charges are variable, depending on the scope of the project. Document delivery charges include: $5 additional per title for next-day rush; same-day rush is $10 additional per title; the lost book fee is $100; rush hourly rate research is $90 plus costs; microform copies are $.25 per page. According to the payment policy, clients may choose a monthly bill, a deposit account, a contract, MasterCard or VISA use. Prepayment is required for foreign accounts.

11. A standard, medium-sized academic library, the collection has such CD-ROM products as *Disclosure, ABI/INFORM, Census Data,* Government Printing Office (*MARCIVE*), *ERIC, Psychlit, SocioFile, MLA, Periodical Abstracts,* and *Newspaper Index.* There is a special collection of municipal publications. The primary services available are online database searching and document delivery. Very limited check-out privileges are available for a $100 deposit fee. Online searching involves a surcharge of $40 an hour, with a $20 minimum. These charges may be billed to the client. Photocopies are self-service at $.05 a copy. There is no request acceptance policy for outsiders.

12. The university offers a Bachelor of Business Administration and several masters degrees in the College of Business Administration. Collections which support these programs are available to anyone in the community for in-house use. Manual searches are limited, but online database searching (at $30. an hour plus vendor connect charge) and interlibrary loan (at $5. plus lending charges) are provided. No book loans are available to members of the business community unless a letter on company letterhead is on file indicating that the employee is conducting research for the company. The fee for this privilege is $25 a year. Photocopies are ten cents per page, with a venda-card the price is reduced to six cents. No fax service is available. Clients are invoiced for online searches.

13. A total collection (reference, general, and special collections) is available, as is the use of government documents (state and local), patents (this is a patent depository library), and the OPAC, including access to bibliographic databases mounted there (some are restricted in the external dial-up node). The services include

literature searching, document delivery, library research, library instruction and orientation, borrowing privileges, and telephone reference service. Circulation, online searching (except for CD-ROM databases), and interlibrary loan are available only by payment of the following fees: for book loans, special borrower cards at $50 a year, or $25 for six months are available for individual use, while corporate borrower rates are negotiated; manual and online searching cost $40 an hour, and for online, vendor and database charges are added; interlibrary loans cost $5 plus lending charges. Other charges include photocopies of university library journal articles for 50 pages and under at $8 plus $.10 a page, which includes copyright royalties; there is an unspecified regular fax service fee in addition to a $.60 per page charge. There is a $2.50 minimum for mail handling and delivery. Such professional services as research, consulting and library instruction cost $40 an hour. Requests from the business community for services normally performed in academic or special library settings are accepted, but policy does not permit patent searches, interpretation of legal or medical data, or the formulation of conclusions based on bibliographic or statistical data. Disclaimers are routinely used. Payment is by billing, except for borrowing privileges for individuals, when payment is expected at the time the card is issued. Purchase orders are accepted, but credit cards are not at this time.

14. Many of the business clients are personnel from corporations which have closed their in-house libraries, and the fee-based service contracts to provide library and information services to these companies. Most of the clients work in science/technology companies located in a business park near the university. These businesses moved to this location because of the compatibility of their interests and the curricula of the university. Full services are provided since this library functions as a "corporate library," performing research, providing document retrieval and delivery, and developing bibliographies for clients and non-clients. Appointments are preferred, but quite a bit of walk-in business is done. All services are provided to anyone, although requests are not usually accepted from the students; students and faculty use the library's reference staff. Manual and online searching charges are $35 an hour for research and online costs—double the price for non-members. Photocopies are $8 per article up to 30 pages, and $.25 for each additional page over this limit; fax service costs $10 plus a rush charge of $10. Book loans are $8 per title. The cost of translation service is negotiated. Clients receive a monthly invoice (30 days net), while non-members who request a major project are required to pay 50% of the cost in advance.

15. The services provided are online database searches, development of subject bibliographies, on-site library management and maintenance, establishment of libraries for companies, translations, compilations of market profiles, document delivery and retrieval, consultations, FAX/Rush service, book and document loans, including interlibrary loans, and manual searching. Business personnel cannot use the CD-ROM databases available to faculty and students. Members of the business community resent this restriction (and complain about it), particularly if their company is a benefactor to the university. Sometimes patrons will request a mediated search of the CD-ROMs to get around the limitation. Manual and online search costs are $35 an hour for members and $65 an hour for non-members; book loans and photocopies are $8 per article (up to 30 pages) for members, and $16 for non-members; fax service is $10 for members and double that for non-members; and fees for translation service are negotiated. Members are billed on a 30 day net basis, while non-members are invoiced, unless the project is an unusually large one; if so, a 50% deposit is required prior to beginning the work.

16. The collection includes directories, CD-ROMs, tax services, corporate reports, a reference and general collection, United States government documents, and much more. Services include document delivery. book loans and photocopies. Outsiders have no access to online searching or interlibrary loan service. A fee of $25 a year is required for a courtesy borrower's card, and a corporate fee of $250 for five cards is also available. Photocopies are $.15 per page; fax costs $4 for the first page, $1 for each additional page, a long distance fee of $5 is also charged when applicable. This library has no request acceptance/payment policy specific to the business community.

17. The library's holdings are extensive, covering all subject areas, including a patents collection, and United States and foreign documents (a depository library). Research services are provided, using manual and online resources, includes document delivery. Clients must open up accounts and abide by copyright limitations. Standard manual and online searching is $75 an hour, rush is $90 an hour; photocopies cost $.15, $.25 or $.35, depending on the turnaround time; local fax service costs $.50 per page, while long distance is double the price. Clients are invoiced monthly, with payment by check only accepted.

Online information retrieval is common to all but one of the responding libraries. Access varies from at least two to as many as ten systems. *DIALOG* is available in all cases, the ability to search the databases on the now defunct *VU/TEXT* system remains for six subscribers, because these files were transferred over to the *DIALOG* system. *BRS* is searchable in twelve libraries, while *LEXIS/NEXIS, Wilsonline,* and *ORBIT* are available in less than half of them. *Dow Jones News Retrieval* (three libraries), *NewsNet* (two libraries), *DataTimes* (two libraries), and *STN* (three libraries) are accessible, along with a variety of other vendor systems in large universities with well developed fee-based services. A state university respondent listed ten online vendors, a CD-ROM network of thirty databases, and a local area network that provides access to library catalogs.

For six respondents, the databases most frequently searched for members of the business community are too numerous to mention, so the subjects covered were provided: business directory information, environment, medical, biomedical, financial, company, geological, engineering, managerial, science/technology, and newspapers.

The most frequently searched database include *ABI/INFORM, Inspec, Compendex, Management Contents, Medline, Predicasts, Chemical Abstracts, Dun's Electronic Business Directory, Trade & Industry Index, Dun's Market Identifiers, PTS Prompt, DIALOG Papers, Predicasts, Magazine Index, Computer Database, Disclosure, Harvard Business Review, Petroleum Abstracts, GeoRef,* and *Toxline.* A respondent from a long-established fee-based service stated that online databases are not usually requested, but the librarian does recommend their use when appropriate.

Since the number of online databases that provide full-text of articles continues to show significant growth, it is not surprising that the requests most often received are for journal articles, valuable for current information of all sorts. Consistent with the frequent use of directory and company databases is the high demand for corporate data. Books and monographs are requested often, illustrating the desire for borrowing privileges by members of the business community.

Research findings for a particular industry or corporation, government documents and reports, and medical, legal, and technical research data are of moderate to high importance. Businesspeople frequently turn to some of the responding libraries for scientific conference proceedings, CD-ROM searching, general interest serials and journals, report writing, addresses, and biographical information.

In summary, the services described readily respond to the needs of their clientele by retrieving and delivering information and documents with as much speed as the user desires—and for a wide range of fees. But just how healthy are these academic library fee-based services?

Eleven of the seventeen respondents indicated that service to the business community increased in both the past and present fiscal years for a variety of reasons, including the following:

- An increase in local software development and health-related products;
- The school has corporate sponsors who may request library service;
- Satisfied customers;
- More and more people are coming in who have lost their jobs due to the recession, and need to find new career opportunities;
- Increased business activity in a rapidly growing metropolitan area; state-industry partnership & technology incubation program starts more agressive marketing on the part of the academic library;
- Service has increased because many companies are reducing the number of services offered in-house to personnel, and are contracting for these. There is a growing trend for corporations to reduce personnel (salaries, benefits, etc.) and hire contract workers to provide library and information services;
- An increase in employee cutbacks and reorganization within local corporations. Several large companies have closed their in-house libraries and the academic library provides these services on a contract basis.

Although this sample is too small to apply the findings to the population at large, it does point to the reasons for the increased demand for fee-based services in institutions with strong research collections.

Even though college and university libraries establish special services to meet the information needs of outsiders, many of whom are members of the business community, they do not tend to actively promote them. Only four of the responding libraries advertise via mass mailings, word-of-mouth, display ads in local directories, listing in telephone directories, newsletter mailings, talks to professional groups, distribution of brochures, membership in groups such as the Chamber of Commerce, and referrals from public libraries.

Only one librarian indicated that service to the business community is evaluated, via a survey currently being conducted. Some comments shed some light on the reasons for not doing so, as follows:

- The service is not formally evaluated, what exactly is done was not specified;
- The administration cannot be convinced of the importance of the business community, even though the public library is inadequate;
- No feedback from the business community is sought, but unspecified statistics on the services provided are collected;
- Referrals and repeat clients are thought to be evidence enough that the library is performing a valuable service to its clients.

If no real effort is made to attract new clients by promoting the service and evaluating its value to outside users, its success and deficiencies cannot be determined. Many factors have to be examined. For example: Does the income cover the service costs—products, space used, telephones, computers, fax machines, photocopiers, online database subscriptions, fees for membership in electronic mail and document delivery systems, networks and more? Are the fees charged for services too high to attract and retain clients? Is the service operated independently, or does it use other library departments and staff for some tasks, such as interlibrary loan? Does this undermine service to the primary clientele? Does the service have its own staff, and is the staff adequate in terms of numbers, training and expertise? Is there sufficient profit for adding or upgrading equipment and services? Has use increased or declined, and what are the reasons?

Since the most important aspect of a fee-based service is document delivery, newer, more efficient and less costly electronic alternatives might narrow the client base, as might emerging, public library services that specifically study and target the local business community.

5

The Public Library- Business Connection: Case Studies

Academic and corporate libraries clearly play an important role as information providers to the business community. Some professionals agree that their collections and services are too strictly guarded, but a conflict very well worth consideration exists. It is difficult to abide by the American Library Association's principle of free and open access for all when staff time, resources, and budget are usually extended to the fullest to meet the needs of the primary clientele—faculty, students, or corporate personnel. As a result, these special libraries tend not to promote service to the general business community because of the fear that demands might negatively affect the fulfillment of the obligation to the members of the institutions they were created to serve. Access is usually controlled in two significant ways to discourage frequent use by outsiders: 1. by appointment only; 2. services made available for a fee.

In contrast, the public library's mission is to provide free and open access to the entire population. But the "free" is in doubt, because substantial costs are involved, including collection development, subscriptions to online database systems, networks, rapid electronic delivery systems, staff and patron training programs, and development of promotional media and methods, etc.

Without a doubt public library information services could play a major role in contributing to the promotion of economic growth, which is greatly dependent on the health of the many information-reliant small businesses established in urban, suburban and rural areas. Library literature reveals that public librarians are beginning to more closely examine their relationships with small businesses, focus on their information needs, and explore methods of providing quality service to this potentially large user group. But how can the public library be promoted as a fully accessible source of vital data necessary for day-to-day business decisions?

A 1984-July study conducted by the Suffolk County Information and Library Service (United Kingdom) revealed that the local business community is generally not aware of available resources, even though some businesspeople do visit or telephone the library.

Interviews conducted with the 43 participating firms uncovered the following:

- Businesspeople lack trust in public library services, believing that requests for technical information cannot be handled with the required degree of accuracy, or within the required time frame;
- They prefer to discuss their information needs with someone who is knowledgeable in their particular field of enterprise—product, operation, finance, marketing, etc.;
- Trade associations and other informal contacts are relied upon because of perceived interest and expertise;
- A visit to the library is necessary only when information is not available via the telephone.

Post-study interviews found that the participants were rather surprised and pleased with the amount of information that can be retrieved, as well as with the accuracy and speed with which it was delivered. The benefits to the businesses included time and money saved, a feeling of security in knowing that the service was available, monetary profit, gaining contracts that they bid for, new clients, and lists of potential customers and suppliers. The service provided had quite an impact, and quickly became valuable for the business community. Another important factor was contact with a known researcher in the library, someone who had visited their companies to promote library service and learn something about each business to be better able to provide for their information needs.

Many of the participants preferred free service but were willing to pay a reasonable fee if necessary. Based on this finding, it was determined that it would be economically and politically advantageous to augment free library service with fee-based information retrieval. Those unwilling or unable to pay would have access to all the services and resources readily accessible to the population served by the library, while clients preferring enhanced, personalized, and quick information retrieval would also be accommodated.[1]

The connection between public libraries and small businesses in Canada was explored by Gwen Zilm in a 1988 *Canadian Library Journal* article. She observed that small businesses generally have a need for information on a wide range of topics specific to a local area, e.g., markets, market research, competitors, management planning, government regulations, financing, patents and patenting, and demographics. The public library can serve as a primary local source for information, as a coordinator of information retrieval, and as a consulting agency for small business personnel. An in-library researcher or information broker (as in the case of the previously mentioned British study) would identify information needs and determine how to best meet them. Local databases, such as business, product, and consultant directories, local newspaper clipping files for background information on markets or industry development and trends on the local level, programs, seminars, and workshops on library resources, manual and end-user information retrieval techniques, small business development and management are effective ways of attracting and retaining clients. A fee-based service for in-depth and personalized research would augment the tax-supported free service.[2]

In 1990 the Iowa City Public Library decided to examine the use of its standard business collection and services to determine how to improve them to meet the growing information needs of local businesses, entrepreneurs, nonprofit, and government organizations.

The research method selected was the focus group, a technique used by market researchers. By definition, focus groups consist of limited numbers of persons brought together to discuss issues of common interest, under the guidance of facilitators who are trained to keep discussions on track.

The issues under consideration at Iowa City were the participants' perceptions of the library, barriers to its use, the level of use of the business collection, alternative information sources available, and methods of improving, expanding, and promoting library services and resources to the business community.

Briefly, the major conclusions drawn from the analysis of the data collected are:

- The library collection is not well used mainly because the business community is not knowledgable about the available resources;
- Promotion of business resources needs to be more energetic and continuous;
- Due to time constraints, some businesspeople do not want to travel to the library, preferring to buy the needed resources or tap other informal sources of information;
- The availability of remote access to services and resources, such as

telephone reference, telefascimile, online access to the library's catalog, and rapid book and document delivery services was thought to be desirable even if charges would be involved;
- Specialized fee-based manual and online information retrieval service for indepth research tailored to individual requirements was suggested.

This focus group project provided a clear view of the information needs of the business community, a comprehensive list of suggestions for improving library service, and an increased awareness, on the part of the participants, of the benefits of using the library.[3]

The following case studies illustrate in detail the importance of improving the business collection to benefit the library, businesses and the local economy, and demonstrate the significance of developing special services that meet the information needs of local businesspeople. Of course, the public library-business community connection is dependent upon staff with expertise, skill, and sustained dedication to providing quality reference and research service to this special clientele.

The Lucy Robbins Welles Library

The Lucy Robbins Welles Library, founded in Newington, Connecticut (Hartford County) in 1752, serves a population of 30,000 with a business community primarily engaged in the manufacture of durable goods, retail trade, finance, insurance, real estate, construction, and professional services mainly in the areas of health and education. The book collection includes 81,851 volumes and 364 periodical subscriptions. Over 350,000 items were circulated in the 1991-92 fiscal year, an increase of 8%; more than 35,000 requests for information were answered in this same year, representing an increase of 18%.

The business collection is quite comprehensive for this medium-sized library. The resources include the following:

- A variety of business magazines and newspapers such as *Barrons, Commercial Record, Business Week, Forbes, Fortune, Harvard Business Review, Inc., Nation's Business, New England Business,* and the *Wall Street Journal;*
- Such business directories as *Directory of Corporate Affiliations, D&B Million Dollar Directory, Directory of New England Manufacturers, MacRae's State Industrial Directory* (for Connecticut), *Standard & Poor's Register of Corporations, Directors and Executives, Thomas Register of American Manufacturers,* and the *Trade Names Directory;*
- A collection of annual reports from major companies located in Connecticut;

- A variety of investment sources, including *Best's Insurance Reports, Moody's Handbook of CommonStocks,* investor service manuals and weekly reports, *Mutual Fund Sourcebook, Standard & Poors/Lipper Mutual Fund Profiles, U.S. Industrial Outlook,* and *Value Line Investment Survey;*
- A selection of commonly used IRS tax forms and reproducible forms from 1984 to the present;
- Such marketing resources as *Editor and Publisher Market Guide, Gale Directory of Publications, RandMcNally Commercial Atlas and Marketing Guide,* and *The Sourcebook of Zip Code Demographics;*
- Local and statewide legal reference tools, including the *BOCA Basic Building Code, General Statutes of Connecticut, Public and Special Acts of the State of Connecticut,* and *Newington Town Ordinances;*
- ther useful sources, such as the *Congressional Directory, Connecticut State Register and Manual,* telephone directories for the state and other major U.S. cities, *Encyclopedia of Associations, Information U.S.A., Federal Regulatory Directory, National Zip Code Directory, OAG Travel Planner: Hotel and Motel Guide, U.S. Government Manual, Washington Information Directory,* and the minutes of the Newington boards and commissions;
- Access to a wide variety of online business databases (via *DIALOG*) that provide bibliographic data, abstracts, full-text, or factual information.

The most frequently used databases are the Dun & Bradstreet files, *Trade & Industry Index, Business Dateline,* and *ABI/Inform.* The types of questions asked are too numerous to mention. There is a limitation of three free searches per week for ready-reference type queries from such databases as *Dun & Bradstreet,* while more detailed free searches are limited to four (up to five minutes) per week per patron. If the search goes beyond the five minute time period allotted, the librarian informs the patron of the estimated cost and negotiates from that point. A budget of $4,400 is allocated for *DIALOG,* and staff is free to search its databases if it is the best way to answer a question. Charges are more likely to be necessary when a patron specifically asks for an online search. Presently, patrons are invoiced, and do not receive the results of the search until payment is made—this arrangement may change if the level of use increases markedly.

All reference staff are trained in the more routine databases, such as Dun & Bradstreet, but three professionals are experienced searchers. A terminal for searching is located at the reference desk, and another one is in the reference office. Staff is sent to every training and update session available to them.

The CD-ROM databases available are *InfoTrac, Newsbank,* and

Books in Print. The library is changing over to CARL Systems, thus increasing the number of databases available via that system. A networked CD-ROM component is planned for the next year.

A telefascimile service is used to send information to the patron if it is the best way to deliver it, but faxing questions to the library is not encouraged because a follow-up reference interview is usually required to clarify what is actually wanted. Acquisition of a coin or credit card operated fax machine that should be quite a handy service for clients who otherwise do not have access to fax machines is being considered. It would also have the capability for a fax "mail box" to store incoming faxes. An option available on the CARL System's *Uncover* database of articles from more than 12,000 journal titles, with over 3,000 new article citations added daily, is that of ordering and receiving copies of the full text of those articles selected by the client via fax within 24 hours using a credit card. The cost includes copyright fees.[3] This type of service would further justify the acquisition of a public fax machine.

Photocopies are $.15 per page. A copyright warning is placed on the copy machine.

The *Newington Business Directory* is a popular in-house database used by many business clients as a direct marketing tool and a quick reference source for local businesses. It can be used in the library, or a copy can be purchased for $25. Mailing labels or listings are available for five cents each. The database records include a number of specific fields, as shown in the following sample record:

Example, Inc.
59 Sample Turnpike
Newington, CT 06111   Year data entered: 1988
111-2222   Year Established: 1941 Fax:
Sales: Employees FT: PT:
Director: Alvin Example
Co-Director:
Parent Co.: n Annual Report: n Chamber Member: y
Business Category: Pet shop
Products/Services: Exotic birds, breeding, boarding, and
          supplies

The Lucy Robbins Welles Library has a tradition of good service. A December 6, 1990 article in the *Hartford Courant* stated that this library provides a variety of services to business owners and job hunters, including a careers collection, materials on resume writing, job interviewing, company financial information, newspaper classified sections, online databases providing access to a wide variety of market and corporate reports, business directories, manufacturers, and more. The small businesses of Newington cannot afford to purchase the resources accessible in the library or pay for costly reference and research services, consultants or counselors. The depressed economy of the past several years, meant that library service to the predominantly small businesses located in Newington needed to be reassessed, as a prerequisite to the commitment to serving the business community. Identification of an effective method of determining the present and future information needs of businesspeople was essential to the library's plan to examine ways of successfully fulfilling those needs. The focus group interview technique was chosen as the best means of gaining insight into the reasons businesspeople do or do not use the library, information that is crucial to increasing the level and quality of library service.

In 1991 the library, with the cooperation of the local Chamber of Commerce, selected businesses and their managers from the four major industries: service, manufacturing, retail trade and construction. Sixty-five letters of invitation were sent out. Telephone calls served as reminders of the planned meetings to those who had agreed to participate and as further enticements to those who had not yet decided to become involved. In the end, 25 people participated among the four focus groups. The meetings were scheduled at the library from 8:00 a.m. to 9:30 a.m. to avoid too great an interference with the workday. Care was taken to keep them informal in order to promote discussion of the questions that arise during the workday, and the sources of information they use to get the answers. The moderator was not a library staff member, but a librarian and business owner who was able to relate to the concerns and experiences of the group members, keep the discussions on track, and encourage group participation. A staff librarian was available during each session to answer any library-related questions and to provide information on the library's services and resources relevant to the members of the four groups.

Analysis of the outcomes of the focus group discussions led to conclusions similar to those of previously discussed studies:

• Businesspeople do not tend to think of the library in relation to their business activities, rather, the library's use is related in their minds to recreational activities;

- Businesspeople do not make the time to make the effort to use the library;
- The value and potential benefits of information to the success of their business was generally not recognized by the participants;
- Technical or industry-specific information is supplied informally by associations, salespersons, government agencies, persons in the same business, outside experts, trade shows, and so forth, the accuracy and dependability of the public library as a source of technical information was doubted;
- Group members were unfamiliar with new technological applications for information retrieval and delivery.

In Newington, the participants learned that the library stands ready to adapt services to suit the needs of its users. It can be a stable, primary resource for the business community, an association for helping with general business concerns, such as marketing, finance, administration and management, a source of information on the use of resources, a training center on the principles of business management for entrepreneurs, a training center for employees, a place to hold various business-related meetings, a source for current awareness information on general or business and industry-specific topics; in short a source of information for specialists and experts in a wide variety of business subjects.

The next step for the Lucy Robbins Welles Library was to sharpen its image as a primary source of information and services relevant to the business community. A business reference pilot program was conducted during March and April, 1992 to further analyze and clarify the perceptions and expectations of businesspeople regarding the delivery of services. Three businesses were paired with three librarians and an information service agreement between the library and the businesses was signed, stating that the companies would request information from the library during the designated two month period. The businesspeople were to record the results of their queries and give an estimate of the value to their businesses of the data received. The librarians were to track the questions asked, the results, and the amount of time spent per query.

A follow-up meeting with the library director was scheduled for evaluating the results of the reference project. While the businesspeople were quite satisfied with the service and information received, the three librarians thought their time limitations would effect the quality of the service and the information retrieved. Other results reported are as follows:

- Some participants preferred photocopies of hard copy sources over paying for a more efficient online search that was likely to yield more relevant and current data.
- Specialized and infrequently used online databases require staff time for study of protocols, search terms, strategies, and so forth prior to going online. The question of whether or not specialization meshes with the goals of a "generalist" medium sized public library needed to be resolved.
- Businesspeople did not naturally turn to the public library for information and felt that there is a real need to actively market library services and resources to both new and established companies.
- The participants appreciated the one-on-one personalized reference service. They felt comfortable dealing with a single librarian who understood their information needs.
- As expected, it was difficult to put a monetary value on the information retrieved for them, with the exception of one business which reported a savings of $1,400. for the two month period.

In June of 1992 an ad hoc advisory committee meeting, which included eight focus group attendees, discussed library services to the business community, focusing on new business-related library activities. The library's commitment to the business community has been reinforced in a variety of ways, as follows:

- In cooperation with the Connecticut Small Business Development Center, the library presented two business programs that included information on library resources, as well as a tour of the business reference area.
- Connecticut Small Business Development Center counselors were introduced to the concept of the library as a valuable source of information, and to the business resources available during a meeting held at the library. Many of the attendees referred their clients to the library.
- A counselor gives free business advice and direction at the library once a week.
- A SCORE (Service Corps of Retired Executives) representative counsels small business personnel at the library once a month.
- The library director serves as library liaison on the executive board of the local Chamber of Commerce.
- A series of four professional development seminars held at the library were planned with the Greater Hartford Community College. Included was information on the resources available in the library that were relevant to the course content.

- The town government, now more than ever before, recognizes the significance of the library to the community as a whole.
- Local businesses donated funds for the purchase of newspaper advertisements for the children's summer reading program as a way of showing their appreciation of what the library has done for them.
- The library publishes a newsletter entitled *Friends In Business*, which provides information on library-business activities, other library programs, services, and special resources, such as the *Newington Business Directory*.

The Lucy Robbins Welles Library has succeeded in convincing businesspeople that it serves as a valuable source of information necessary for economic success. In order to further increase the number of business clients, the library applied for and received an LSCA grant to fund a program that will study methods of achieving even closer interaction with local businesses. Library staff will visit 50 local businesses, representative of those in the Newington area, to introduce them to library services and resources, answer their business-related questions, and gather pertinent data about their information needs in order to enhance the business collection to meet these needs, increase information delivery time and fill rate. This outreach program, scheduled to begin in 1993, should meet with the same success as the previous programs because of the energy and serious commitment of the library's director and staff.[4]

Commerce Public Library

The City of Commerce Public Library, Commerce, California, serves a population of 12,500. Since its founding in 1961, its Central Library and two branches have been providing library service to the large "business resident" population (80%), as well as a general resident population (20%), consisting of 40% high school graduates (two-thirds Spanish-speaking), with a median household income of $27,415. Over time the types of businesses changed from manufacturing to warehousing and service industries. In fiscal year 1990-91, 153,227 items were circulated in the library.

The book collection consists of 100,000 volumes and 300 magazine subscriptions. Abundant government revenue resources have allowed this library to acquire business resources not normally available in a small public library. They include the following:

- A variety of business magazines and newspapers such as *Aviation Week, Advertising Age, Barrons, BusinessWeek, California Business, California State Contracts Register, Chain Store Age, Entrepreneur,*

Forbes, Fortune, Harvard Business Review, Industry Week, Los Angeles Business Journal, Nation's Business, Personnel Journal, Working Woman, Wall Street Journal;
- Such business directories as *Brands and Their Companies, Building and Construction Blue Book, California Manufacturers Register, California Services Register, Consulting and Consulting Organizations Directory, Directory of Corporate Affiliations, Dun & Bradstreet Million Dollar Directory, Los Angeles Business Directory, MacRAE's Blue Book, National Fax Directory, Southern California Business Directory and Buyer's Guide, Standard and Poor's Register, Standard Directory of Advertising, Thomas Register of Manufacturers, Ward's Business Directory;*
- A selection of financial services such as *Moody's Manuals, Daily Graphs-American & New York Stock Exchange, Value Line Investment Survey and Ratings and Reports, Standard & Poor's Corporation Records, Trendline,* and various stock reports;
- Such small business resources as *Consumer Price Index, Small Business Sourcebook, Starting and Operating a Business in California, The Franchise Annual, SBA Hotline Answer Book,* and *How to Set Up Your Own Small Business;*
- Career information sources, such as the *Dictionary of Occupational Titles, American Almanac of Jobs and Salaries, Occupational Outlook Handbook;*
- A variety of resume and job hunting handbooks, company information, journals, and other resources for the job seeker, such as state and national directories of trade and professional associations, and job interview and search titles.

Because there is little demand for online searching, this service is not available in-house. But for those who require access to databases, it is available at a discount, negotiated by the library with a local vendor for all city businesses. This arrangement has only recently been publicized. Automated information retrieval is available at the Central Library via *InfoTrac*—700 of the magazines indexed are accessible on microfilm for fast retrieval.

A variety of services to assist the business community are listed in a brochure entitled, *"Business Help"*. These services reflect the close geographical relationship between the library and the community. Traveling to the Central Library or its two branches does not involve the inconvenience of distance in order to use any of the following:

- Free public access computers (PACS) available by reservation or on a first-come-first served basis;
- Typewriters;

- Self-service copy machines, at a cost of ten cents per page;
- Work tables for use as an alternative work site for those who need to work away from the office, to spread their work out, use their own calculators or laptop computers;
- A collection of recorded books or video cassettes;
- The twenty-four hour book drop.

Requests for material or information can be delivered via fax. A valuable service provided for clientele is spelling assistance.

The reference staff devotes liberal time periods to individual clients in order to provide them with the needed information and resources. When a title is not held, OCLC is searched. Referrals are readily made to appropriate organizations, associations, consultants, or government agencies. In an effort to further enhance service, a list of possible members for a Business Friends of the Library is planned for the next year.

A part-time (twelve hours per week) business liaison librarian was just recently designated because it had been discovered that beyond demographic data little information about the changing business community was known. Heavy manufacturing was replaced by warehousing and service industries, and the needs of these new residents had to be identified and accommodated. After a letter of introduction was sent to new businesses, the liaison librarian arranged to meet with the person who signed the business license to announce the availability of library resources and services (listed in the brochures given out) that might be beneficial to the particular enterprise, and to determine what services and resources, if any,are currently used or might be added to the collection. As a result of the meetings the need for English as a second language materials, and for information on small business resources were identified. Two brochures will be developed to promote use of the library for information and materials covering these two areas.

A *JOBS* (Jobs, Opportunities, Business, Sources) table was created during the recession. Job seekers may use reference copies of job listings, resume books, salary information, the *Occupational Outlook Handbook*, etc. more, that are placed on this table.

The City of Commerce Public Library actively spreads the word about the value of the library—its staff, collection, and services—with well designed brochures. It also has a cooperative relationship with the Los Angeles Society for Coatings Technology, whereby the society donates titles to the collection. In return, the library prepares an annual bibliography of holdings significant to the society's membership. The library is also promoted via a monthly column written by the city public information officer and published in *Strictly Business,* an official publication of the Industrial Council-Chamber of Commerce, which sometimes features information on the library's services and resources.[6]

The City of Commerce Public Library has succeeded in convincing many businesspeople of its value as a source of information essential to their growth and vitality. These efforts to define and satisfy the different information needs of a changing clientele should lead to an even further enhanced business collection that is tailor-made to serve a changing business community.

The Cleveland Public Library

The Cleveland Public Library, founded in 1869, serves a population of 505,616, with a book collection of 2,433,685 volumes and 5,591 periodical subscriptions. Over five million items were circulated in the 1991 fiscal year.

The Cleveland Research Center, a fee-based information service agency of the Cleveland Public Library was started in 1987. It serves the business community locally, within the state, and out of state, and is most frequently used by corporate personnel. Personnel of small- and medium-sized businesses, entrepreneurs, researchers, and technicians use the service moderately, while corporate and public library staff, job-seekers, and college and university students are not very significant client groups. Government officials are infrequent users, perhaps because their information needs are directly met by resources within their own offices and libraries.

Through the Cleveland Research Center, businesspeople have access to the full range of materials in the library's collection: over 2,000 online databases, experts within industry, government, and nationwide information centers via networks. The sources include investment house reports, local and national newspapers, popular magazines, trade journals, industry newsletters, conference proceedings, financial reports, new product announcements, import and export listings, government documents, wire services, annual reports, legislative histories, patents, trademarks, directories, industry standards, and more. In addition, a complement of data resources is used to tailor projects to meet the needs of individual clients.

The resources most frequently requested by members of the business community are journal articles, corporate data, research findings for a particular industry or corporation, and online databases. Government documents and reports are requested with somewhat less frequency, while medical, legal, and technical research data, and the opinions of experts in various fields are in moderate demand. Books and monographs are the least requested materials.

A wide variety of online services are available—*BRS, DIALOG, Dow Jones News Retrieval, Lexis/Nexis, ORBIT, VU/TEXT* (its databases now available only via *DIALOG*), *WILSONLINE*, *Hannah Legislative Tracking Service*, *OHIOPI*, *Dun & Bradstreet* and *Dun & Bradstreet Business Information Reports*, *Cleveland Newspaper Index*, and *DataTimes*. The databases most frequently searched are those available on *DIALOG*, *DOW JONES*, and *Lexis/Nexis;* the individual databases are too numerous to mention.

Online searching is done at cost, while the charge for manual searching is $60 per hour, and $90 per hour for rush service. The price varies for information tracking or current awareness service. Photocopies are ten cents per page plus tax. A policy change is pending with regard to fax charges. Other charges include translation service which is done at cost; Dun & Bradstreet Report at $60 each; $2 each for long-distance calls; and document delivery, via fax, mail, courier, personal computer networks, overnight mail, pick-up window or telephone, at cost.

Request deposits are required, but VISA, MASTERCARD, or purchase order numbers are used as retainers. Clients are billed via credit cards, or they are invoiced, with payment due within thirty days.

Services, including manual research, online searching, telephone queries, and information tracking (current awareness), are not limited to special groups, nor are limits imposed on access to library materials beyond policy guidelines. Research is conducted in an ethical manner, with data sought from suppliers considered public, not proprietary. Clients are asked to make appointments whenever possible.

Service to the business community has increased in the past fiscal year because of increased awareness of the service and referrals from clients. Evaluation is done on a monthly basis by analyzing such reports as the amount invoiced, the amount of income, year-to-date invoiced figure, year-to-date income, and the number of requests received.

The comprehensive collection of the Business, Economics and Labor Department covers statistics, economics, management, real estate, labor, industries, transportation, communications, marketing, accounting, salestechnique, advertising, finance, insurance, public finance, banking, and taxation.

This department maintains the following special resources:

- A microfiche collection of annual reports, 10K and proxy statements for all SEC filing companies, as well as *Moody's, Standard & Poors*, and *ValueLine;*
- Trade and manufacturing directories, telephone directories for major United States cities and selected international areas, and trade directories;
- Foreign trade sources for export and import business information, and such handbooks as the *International Marketing Handbook;*

- Business indexes, such as *Business Periodicals Index, Predicast's F&S Corporations Index, Accountants Index,* and *Work Related Abstracts;*
- Investment and securities services—*Merrill Lynch Newsletter, Trendline, ValueLine, Standard & Poor's Outlook, Standard & Poor's Statistical Service, Crandall's Business Index/Interindustry Forcasts,* etc.;
- An extensive collection of labor and employment resources
- Business-related periodicals;
- Small business materials—labor law, payroll deduction, sales compensation, marketing, taxes, trade directories, manuals for starting and managing a small business;
- Tax services, security values, tax rate sources, materials on mergers and acquisitions.

Clients have access to company information via personal computers and CD-ROM products such as *InfoTrac, ABI/Inform,* and *Moody's 5000 Plus.* The staff also does quick reference searches on *DIALOG* databases.

Coin-operated self-service photocopy machines are available for client convenience.

The Cleveland Research Center is actively marketed to the business community, using such media as radio, print ads, presentations and direct mail. In addition, the library's Business, Economics and Labor Department prepares bibliographies of holdings that are of current significance. For example, *Women & Entrepreneurship, Direct Marketing, Information and Resources,* and *Small Business Resources* are evidence that this established urban library analyzes patron needs and collection adequacy continuously to keep up with the changing information needs of the business community. The level of commitment to serving this large and varied group of special clients is consistently high in Cleveland.[7]

The Memphis/Shelby Public Library

The Memphis/Shelby Public Library and Information Center, founded in 1893, serves a population of 828,082 with a collection of 1,499,018 book volumes. The library participates in the South Eastern Library Network and has access to *DIALOG* and *Dow Jones News-Retrieval.* In 1992, 2,587,331 titles were circulated.

Its Science/Business/Social Science Department has two recently organized collections: The First Tennessee Small Business Center and the Job and Career Center, due to an increasing demand from the public for information about starting a business or searching for a job. They are still new collections—the former opened in February 1992, and the later in September 1991.

The Small Business Center was created with $20,000 in start-up money targeted to cover the cost of equipment, the collection, promotion and printing. During the ordering process it became evident that the maintenance of a useful collection would require more funding from an outside source. The library found the corporate sponsorship it sought, and formed a unique partnership with the First Tennessee Bank to provide a valuable resource, referral, and distribution center.

The up-to-date collection includes books, audiotapes, videotapes, and periodicals that are aimed at small business needs, particularly for those interested in starting a business. The sources cover the following topics:

- Projections and outlook—including *Standard and Poor's Industrial Survey, Valuline Investment Survey, Standard Industrial Classification Manual, Almanac of Business and Industry Financial Ratios;*
- Referral agencies and resources/networking—some titles listed are *Where to go for Small Business Information, Encyclopedia of Associations, State and Regional Associations of the United States, Encyclopedia of Business Information Sources, Small Business Sourcebook, The Halbert Guide to Financial Newsletters;*
- Market information for business plans—with such titles as *RMA Annual Statement Studies, Almanac of Business and Industrial Financial Ratios, Standard and Poor's Industry Surveys, Financial Studies of the Small Business,* U.S. and state economic censuses, *Agricultural Census, County Business Patterns, Wall Street Journal Index;*
- Demographics—including *Donnelley's Demographics, CACI Sourcebook of Zip Code Demographics/County Demographics;*
- Sources of supply and customers—such as *Who's Who in Memphis Business, Doing Business in Memphis, Memphis Manufacturers Directory, Dun & Bradstreet Million Dollar Directory, Standard and Poor's Register,* state manufacturing directories, *Thomas Register of Manufacturers*
- State and local restrictions—including *Starting and Operating a Business in Tennessee, Steps to Starting a Business in Memphis & Shelby County, Tennessee Small Business Information,* and city and county laws and ordinances;
- Patent and trademark information—including government documents and resources on patents and trademarks, trademark computer search and other resources;
- Financial sources—such as *Catalog of Federal Domestic Assistance, Handbook for Raising Capital, Small Business Loan Kit, SBA Loans: A Step By Step Guide;*
- How-to books on a variety of business topics from accounting to valuation;

- How-to books on specific types of businesses, such as catering, craft, freelancing, janitorial, and restaurant/bed and breakfast.

Databases are available for in-house use only and include the Commerce Department's *National Trade Data Bank* and the *SBA's Business Disc*, an interactive laser disk that takes the potential entrepreneur through the steps involved in starting a business, indicating whether the business decisions made along the program's route would lead to success. The user must first complete the required research and planning steps, including business goals, plan of action and funding. The two-part program is a simulation of a first year of business that takes from five to ten hours to complete. A workbook and formatted disk are required, and are available for purchase for $6.

The Small Business Center is used as a clearinghouse of information from area non-profit agencies that offer services to small businesses and entrepreneurs, and referrals are readily made to sources of assistance in the Memphis area via a small business agency referral network. Each agency was contacted and interviewed by two members of the Science/Business Department, which resulted in two-page descriptions of each agency in a booklet entitled, "Where to Go for Small Business Information." The entries include information on what each agency does, eligibility requirements, hours, the names of contact persons, and a subject index.

Science/Business staff regularly attend meetings of the Memphis Chamber of Commerce Small Business Council to maintain contact with the business community and to gain information about subjects of concern. The Small Business Center's services are promoted via a variety of brochures and handouts, such as a listing of sources of information by subject, an informational sheet on *Business Disc*, an informational/bibliographic flyer on materials located in the Small Business Center designed to help a client consider, start, and run a small business, an annotated bibliography of demographic resources, and a two-page informational handout on steps to starting a small business from the Shelby County Clerk's Office Business Taxation Division. Included is brief information, names, addresses, and telephone numbers for obtaining a business tax licence in certain cities; a certificate of use and occupancy; the county certificate of use and occupancy, the county sign ordinance; the personal property tax, and more.

The Center is open seven days a week—9 A.M. to 9 P.M. Monday-Thursday, 9 A.M. to 6 P.M. Friday-Saturday, and 1-5 P.M. on Sunday.

The library has five Job and Career Centers—one at the main library, and four in branches. The resources available include reference and circulating books, periodicals, videos and vertical file materials about a variety of careers, career selection and changing, and job searching strategies.

This service is promoted via an informational flier, and a listing of the types of sources available and titles useful for locating descriptive and financial data on corporations. Tours of the Job Center are conducted at the main library when requested by groups. Some have been given for high school and college classes, but the majority are for re-careering support groups whose members are interested in learning how to use library resources to assist them in their job-seeking efforts.

A related outreach service is the JobLinc Van, a division of the Information & Referral Department. Its purpose is to make job-readiness information available to the community by delivering it directly to the people. A staff of specialists is on board to assist job seekers obtain information necessary to obtaining, keeping, and advancing in a job. A collection of books, audiotapes, videotapes, computer programs and LINC files of community training programs and educational resources is available for this purpose.

An informational flyer that describes JobLinc and how it works is used to promote the service, along with two very useful small fliers— a list of hotline numbers that provide recorded messages of job openings and how to apply for the positions, and a list of agencies in Memphis that may offer day labor in such jobs as warehouse, general labor, light industrial, material handler, stocker, packer, and forklift driver.

Yet another service, The Library Channel, airs such programs as *Jobfile: Job Listings from the State Office of Employment Security, Library Linc, Employment Security Works,* and *Small Business Review.*[8]

The Memphis/Shelby County Public Library is a key player in the effort to link the business/jobless community to information vital to growth and success—thereby significantly influencing the economic future of the area.

NOTES

1. Fiona Trott and John Martyn, "An Information Service for Small Firms from a Public Library Base," *ASLIB Proceedings* 38 (February 1986): 43-50.

2. Gwen Zilm, "Meeting the Needs of Canada's Small Businesses," *Canadian Library Journal* 45 (April 1988): 109-12.

3. Sharon L. Baker, "Improving Business Services Through the Use of Focus Groups," *RQ* 30 (Spring 1991): 377-85.

4. Further information on CARL Systems can be obtained by contacting them: 3801 E. Florida Avenue, Bldg D, Suite 300, Denver, Colorado 80210; Telephone: 303-758-3030.

5. Information on the Lucy Robbins Welles Library was generously provided by Maxine Bleiweis, Director.

6. Information on the City of Commerce Public Library was generously provided by Dr. Carrie Coolbaugh, Assistant Director.

7. Information on the Cleveland Public Library's services was generously provided by Angela Baughman Bowie, Cleveland Research Center.

8. Information on the services of the Memphis/Shelby County Public Library and Information Center was generously provided by Kay Cunningham, Science/Business/Social Science Department.

6

Expanding Service Dimensions

Many public librarians may believe that they are providing the business community with the best information and reference service possible, considering that access to resources is governed by budget constraints and administrative decisions based on a perception of the value of the service in relation to other library functions and services. Many librarians claim they are too busy to monitor the level of service provided to businesspeople, and put the emphasis on doing and making do without analyzing the level of satisfaction of the clients who use the library as a business-related information resource. The pressures to perform in this way are great, but it is a short-sighted policy. Clearly, corporate librarians quickly learn that inadequate evaluation leads to the loss of company support, and the downsizing or discontinuance of the library in favor of outside services that are able to deliver the data needed in an efficient and dynamic way. Likewise, public library professionals try to resist being governed by the crisis mentality brought on by persistent funding deficiencies.

Once the commitment to provide quality reference service is made, qualitative and quantitative analysis of what is being done and what cannot but should be done to provide optimum service to the business community as imperative. The development of a current and accurate profile of the business community, and an examination of the possibilities for service enhancement through access to electronic media are first steps. Such evaluation is the key to gaining more personnel, the use of automated information retrieval systems, network access, staff and client training programs, necessary equipment, an improved collection of books, periodicals and other hard copy sources, programs to meet the needs of a variety of business client groups, expanded library hours, support for long-term study of the business population and its present and future information needs, partnerships with business leaders, and more. Businesspersons know information is power, but many do not realize that public libraries offer value-added service and the means to free and affordable access to both manual and computer-mediated services vital to economic success.

For the most part the questionnaire respondents indicated that some evaluation is considered significant, but the lack of any evaluatory procedures, an inconsistent approach, or the collection of only one or two types of data results in little progress in expanding the dimensions of service to the business community. The use of statistical and descriptive data guides the development and enhancement of services, provides verification of the need to acquire resources in all formats, and clarifies goals, policies and procedures. An integral part of the professional's job is to compare and contrast a variety of hard data to prove that there is a need for change in order to enhance information and reference service to the business community.

The data that we believe should be collected and analyzed, includes the following:

- The number of questions answered and not answered: to analyze the adequacy and currency of the collection; staff knowledge of the resources; the need for access to more rapid and current electronic resources, reference interview skills; staff and client knowledge of reference skills; the ease of use of hard copy or computerized resources; usefulness of the resources used; and staff responsiveness to individual requests.
- Sources used to answer individual questions: to test the adequacy and currency of the collection and the information retrieved; discover staff awareness of alternative sources; referral activity, and the level of service provided.
- Number of CD-ROM and online database searches run and the success rate or rate of accuracy: to study the ease of use of CD-ROMs by staff and clients; the appropriateness of automated systems with regard to user needs; analysis of mediated online searching policies, procedures, restrictions; the affordability of fees charged for services; the adequacy of the collection; staff expertise level; effectiveness of staff and client training programs; justification of additional online vendor subscriptions or CD-ROM products; staff ability to create accurately targeted search strategies; assessment of database content; search protocols, and the need for budget revision to accommodate the demand for electronic information retrieval.
- User satisfaction as determined by interview or quesionnaire results: to study staff success rate; the ability to analyse search results, in-

terpret search requests and results; the relevancy and timely delivery of information; the need for additional resources; the adequacy of staff training in the use of reference resources; the level of staff interaction with individual business clients; the effectiveness of service for the in-person, telephoning, or faxing client; staff responsiveness to various levels of queries; the effectiveness of staff instruction; and to analyze the population served by polling area businesses regarding information needs.

- The results of studies of the use of networks and resource sharing: to examine cooperative relationships with other libraries and types of libraries, and membership in cooperative networks to determine the degree of use and usefulness, and the adequacy of the collections; sources most requested and success rate; to justify staff time for developing cooperative relationships; the effectiveness of cooperative links in terms of the transfer of information and the willingness to reciprocate in resource sharing.
- Analysis of interlibrary loan requests and requests filled: to determine collection strengths and weaknesses; the correctness of acquisitions decisions; the accuracy of the materials selection policy; the funds allocated for hard copy and automated resources; and the speed of information delivery via various avenues.
- The number of referrals to special libraries and types of libraries used: to analyze the adequacy of the available resources; the fill rate from other libraries; the success of resource sharing and cooperative links; the reasons for referrals; staff response to clients in need of referrals; staff knowledge of outside resources and access policies of other libraries; the quality of service provided to obtain information for clients; and the reasons for referrals, i.e., to obtain journal articles, specialized hard copy sources, online database access.
- Assessment of collection development policy and procedure: to study staff knowledge of the information needs of the business community and the ability to meet those needs; to consider reallocation of funds for the acquisition of CD-ROM or online database systems to meet the demand for rapid delivery of current data; and to explore expanding the collection to cover local needs as well as requests for information on the global marketplace.

Evaluation clearly requires a strong commitment to the continuous assessment of the users of the business collection, indepth study of the business community and potential users, and constant examination of every aspect of service to businesspeople. Gathering and analyzing data takes time, but without this data, public librarians will not be able to confirm that information needs are being met or to prove that not meeting them is a serious deficiency for the economic life of the community.

Quality information and reference service cannot be offered if professionals do not quickly realize that technology will not cause librarian obsolescence. We will survive if we embrace the new, expanded, and vital role electronic information retrieval and delivery presents to us, and work hard to fully understand the potential of technology as an efficient means of fulfilling certain needs of our clients accurately and efficiently.

Many information professionals have advocated the introduction of mediated searching, CD-ROM databases, end-user searching, easy access to library holdings via online public access catalogs, adding value to these OPACs via 24 hour remote access, and by mounting leased tapes of commercial databases onto them—all in the name of better service.

The way information is accessed and delivered has changed dramatically as technology has evolved. Bibliographic data, full-text articles, complete books, and images can travel from one part of the world to another with great speed, and information of all kinds can be quickly transmitted via the communications highways of the Internet. Fax, electronic and voice mail have become more significant methods of information exchange than the telephone and the traditional mail route, and are commonplace in large and small business offices. Given the equipment, businesspeople in rural areas can have the same access to as wide a variety of information sources as are accessible in urban centers. The use of these information retrieval and communications technologies depends upon knowledge and training in effective utilization of them. It is up to the information professional to make clients aware of the possibilities and to develop ways of connecting them with the data to satisfy corporate and individual business information needs. This task is not a new one. Information professionals have been evaluating end-user product design, database content, online search protocols, the accuracy of search results, and more for some time. Many clients fail to understand online searching, or do not have the interest, time or money to try to learn how to use online information retrieval systems. They will continue to rely on the expertise of professionals for mediated searching or for assistance in learning the process themselves. Furthermore, businesspeople are not likely to be able or willing to keep up with the vast amount of information resources available. In order to provide quality service, the librarian's role as intermediary, connecting clients to information, and guiding them through electronic highways, is multifaceted. The following characterizes the major responsibilities of the true information professional:

• Assuming a leadership role in advocating the use of technology by library professionals and members of the business community;

- Gaining indepth knowledge of the field in order to evaluate the usefulness of various products, becoming involved in the development and use of new technologies and product enhancements, and being able to explain the use and value of computer systems to clients;
- Conducting expert mediated online searches, interpreting information requests, analyzing, evaluating and packaging information in a form that is useful for clients, and delivering the information as quickly as possible;
- Becoming an information consultant with the ability and skill to select appropriate paths to information retrieval, create new information services that are tailor-made for business clients, evaluate client needs and business data resources available, develop knowledge of local businesses and rapport with individual businesspeople in order to accurately meet their needs, and to gain the knowledge of database pricing, access costs, copyright problems and charges in order to retrieve data in the most cost-effective manner;
- Educating librarians and end-users in the effective use of resources, guiding users through the research process, anticipating future needs by studying market and industry trends;
- Marketing library use—remote access via telephone, fax or computer, as well as the availability of rapid personalized service, to gain the attention and support of the business community, government officials, and the library administration;
- Gaining expertise in navigating LANs (local area networks), WANs (wide area networks), state and regional cooperative networks and the INTERNET—anticipating wider use of this worldwide system of interconnected networks, by learning what is available and how to easily get at it.
- Examining the budget problem that prevents access to computer systems and lobby for reform and additional funding from government and private sources so that libraries might gain full access to the rapidly growing body of information in electronic format. Work to establish a budget for computerized information retrieval by tracking expenditures and anticipating additional costs for hardware, software, documentation, system upgrades, personnel, and more.

The need for a partnership of information professionals, library administrators, local, state, and federal government, and the philanthropic community is essential to the expansion of business information and reference service that fully utilizes technology as well as traditional services and resources. The effort to provide full access to information to the entire population may seem futile, considering persistent fiscal crises, and the related decreases in public library budgets. But it is possible to create a state-of-the-art library if it is made clear to all involved that the services resources will help boost the economy by promoting efficient access to vital data.

An example of the feasability of such an undertaking is the New York Public Library's $100 million project to build the country's largest public science, industry, and business library and information center. In addition to the library's own financing commitment, millions of dollars are being sought and pledged by the city, the state of New York, the federal government and the private sector, ncluding corporations, foundations and individuals.

The resources, covering a wide range of subjects from advertising to zoology, will include an extensive research collection of over 2.5 million volumes; an open-shelf reference collection of over 60,000 items; a circulating collection of 80,000 books; over 110,000 business and scientific journals and periodicals; electronic business and scientific resources via dial-access, CD-ROM, and tape-loaded files; a comprehensive collection of United States and foreign government documents, patents, industrial directories and buyer's guides; extensive international trade resources, technical reports, standards and codes; domestic and foreign corporate annual reports in hard copy, microform and electronic formats; financial information services, such as newsletters, stock reporting and loose-leaf services; and basic texts and reference works.

The population served will include a diverse national and international clientele, but it will also fully utilize information technology to provide a variety of services to small businesses, entrepreneurs, corporations, researchers and secondary school, college and university students. These include the following:

- Access to global information via the INTERNET for remote users as well as on-site users/gateways to INTERNET databases, electronic journals and bulletin boards;
- An electronic information center with one hundred work stations;
- An electronic information training center with 26 work stations to assist the public in the use of computer resources;
- Document delivery, 24 hour dial-in access, E-mail, and telephone reference service;
- Small business information service, offering guidance to resources for the development of business plans, management methods, markets, legal issues, and government assistance programs;
- An international trade resource center to help clients compete in the global marketplace, providing access to international import and export data, foreign markets (particularly Asia, Latin America and the European Economic Community), and government regulations;
- Formally initiated partnerships with secondary schools, college and

universities to create science education programs in which the library will have a major role as the primary resource for information and reference;
- Value-added fee-based services to accommodate the needs of the business community for in-depth research, extensive online searches, tailor-made information retrieval projects and rapid document delivery.

This new library, scheduled for a 1995 opening, will break down the barriers of access to computer technology (for example, lack of equipment, knowledge, and training) by providing easy access to data via electronic means in response to the changing needs of a changing business environment.

But New York City is a large urban center of business, finance, and industry that includes a private sector of corporate giants, foundations and individual philanthropists to provide the monetary support for such an impressive project. Is it possible, in this era of fiscal misery, to improve access to information in areas where fewer resources, minimal staffing, and less staff trained in the use of electronic information retrieval are commonplace? Just how can a wide variety of information be made available through small libraries?

The answer lies in statewide leadership to establish cooperative arrangements with commercial database producers; to create, maintain, and distribute government and state-created databases; develop staff training programs on the use of electronic resources and networks; provide gateways to database searching and the necessary communications networks for library or patron access to a state information network, with a connection to the INTERNET; to subsidize the communications costs for users; distribute the software needed for CD-ROM and online access; and to evaluate state-wide service for the purpose of upgrading, enhancing and solving problems of access, database quality, ease of use, and more. This level of state involvement is feasible. For example, Access Colorado is a network committed to providing free access to the information resources of the libraries of the state, as well as those resources in other computerized databases, for the support of educational, health, social service and business needs of all Colorado residents.

The Colorado legislature created the Access Colorado network by authorizing the Colorado State Library to raise monies to develop and operate a network that would link library (primarily catalogs) and information databases, providing toll-free dial-in access from libraries or any other place a user has the necessary equipment at hand. The state library administers Access Colorado, but participant concerns and suggestions are considered by an advisory committee for policy and planning. A technical committee is involved in network design, and a training and support committee is responsible for the development of a training program, documentation, and customer services.

Small businesses, rural entrepreneurs, and others in need of business information can benefit from free access to this information network by the use of a wide variety of resources not otherwise available, by learning to use computers to locate information, and by realizing the benefits of competition in the national or global marketplace.

With persistent interest, promotion, and lobbying efforts, such state networks as Access Colorado have the potential to provide as wide a variety of services and resources as are available in large urban areas.

The nature of access methods and the availability of electronic resources depends on the ever-evolving online industry. Technological developments have resulted in big changes in accessibility, but free access via local, regional, and national networks, as well as the network of networks—INTERNET will not be realized for a time because of copyright problems and a variety of pricing issues (i.e., database use charges, royalty fees, and telecommunications costs) that must be resolved. Free library service is not really free. Even though the cost may not be apparent to the end-user, somebody has to pay the bill. The dimensions of service can be expanded only if budgets expand. Federal, state and local government subsidies are as necessary as private sector support. But the total commitment and initiative of information professionals to improving service to the business community is of the greatest significance in making it happen.

Appendix A
Survey of Public Library Business Information and Reference Services

A. GENERAL INFORMATION

1. Is professional staff available to provide business reference and information service: (check as many as apply)
   - ____ a. evenings?
   - ____ b. Saturdays?
   - ____ c. Sundays?

2. Please rate on a scale numbered from 1-5 the frequency of use of the business and information service by the following user groups:
   - ____ corporate personnel
   - ____ personnel of small or medium size businesses
   - ____ entrepreneurs or self-employed
   - ____ researchers or technicians
   - ____ government officials
   - ____ corporate library staff
   - ____ academic library staff
   - ____ job seekers
   - ____ students
   - ____ special interest groups
   - ____ other (please specify) _____
   _____

B. COLLECTION

3 . Which of the following best describes the arrangement of your business collection? (check one)

_____ a. business information center located in the main library

_____ b. separate business library located in or near the business district

_____ c. other (please specify) _____

4. Does the business information and reference collection include: (check as many as apply)

_____ a. dictionaries, encyclopedias

_____ b. subject specific indexes

_____ c. government documents

_____ d. company reports, corporate data

_____ e. industry data, statistics, trends

_____ f. general newspapers, journals

_____ g. subject and industry-specific newspapers, journals

_____ h. newspaper clipping file

_____ i. newsletters

_____ j. local and state regulations and reports

_____ k. doctoral dissertations and theses

_____ l. legal indexes, dictionaries, encyclopedias

_____ m. patent and trademark data

_____ n. employment/occupation resources

_____ o. other (please specify) _____

_____

If your library has a written collection policy, please send a copy.

C. SERVICES

5. Which of the following services are available to business information and reference service users? (check as many as apply)

_____ a. ready-reference service (including photocopy)

_____ b. retrieval of hard-to-find or obscure information

_____ c. mediated online database searching (librarian searches)

_____ d. end-user searching of online databases (patron searches)

_____ e. editing of downloaded search results prior to delivery in printed or electronic formats

_____ f. SDI service (Selective Dissemination of Information), or monthly updates on specific topics, including bibliographic data and abstracts.

_____ g. interlibrary loan for items not in the collection
_____ h. bibliographies of new items in the business field
_____ i. telephone reference service
_____ j. telefacsimile service
_____ k. training programs on available resources, the use of
the collection, and end-user searching
_____ l. other (please specify) _____

6. What restrictions are placed on the available services? For example, time limitations, time spent per question, type of information requested, call-backs.

7. Are patrons referred from the business information and reference service to other departments of your library for answers to questions covering other subject areas? ____yes ____no

8. Does your library actively market business information and reference service? ____yes ____no

If yes, is it promoted by such media as: check as many as apply)
_____ a. library newsletter
_____ b. newspaper ads or articles
_____ c. radio, television
_____ d. bookmarks, flyers, posters
_____ e. exhibits at business and industry fairs and conventions
_____ f. subject bibliographies
_____ g. lists of new acquisitions
_____ h. direct mail campaigns
_____ i. special fee-based research service for corporate personnel
_____ j. other (please specify) _____
_____

D. COOPERATION AND CORPORATE LIBRARIES

9. Which libraries do you cooperate with? (check as many as apply)
_____ a. corporate libraries
_____ b. college or university libraries
_____ c. association libraries
_____ d. other public libraries
_____ e. other (please specify) _____
_____

10. Do you refer patrons to corporate libraries? ____yes ____no

   If yes, do you (check as many as apply)
   ____ a. give name, location and library hours?
   ____ b. librarian calls referral library to arrange for patron visit?
   ____ c. librarian calls the referral library to explain request to corporate librarian?
   ____ d. librarian obtains information from corporate library and delivers it to patron?
   ____ e. other (please specify) _____

   _____

11. Please rate on a scale numbered from 1-5 the resources which are most frequently requested from corporate libraries? (least 1-2-3-4-5 most)
   ____ books or monographs related to individual requests not available in your library
   ____ articles from journals not available in your library
   ____ data on particular corporations
   ____ information on research findings in a particular industry or corporation
   ____ medical, legal, technical research data
   ____ special indexes, bibliographies, dictionaries
   ____ government documents/reports
   ____ online databases not available in your library or not searched
   ____ CD-ROM databases not available in your library
   ____ other (please specify) _____

   _____

12. Do corporate libraries impose service limitations on the patrons you refer to them? ____yes ____no

   If yes, please explain:

13. Has cooperation with corporate libraries increased:
   a. in the past fiscal year? ____yes ____no
   b. in this fiscal year?   ____yes ____no

   If yes, what are the reasons? (check as many as apply)

	Past Fiscal	This Fiscal
inadequate budget, rising cost of materials	_____	_____
need for reference resources not available in the library	_____	_____

	Past Fiscal	This Fiscal
corporate library fills information needs rapidly and thoroughly	_____	_____
greater demand for a variety of journals located using online databases	_____	_____
membership in cooperative networks and the expected resource sharing and reciprocation	_____	_____
corporate library listings in library directories	_____	_____
other (please specify)	_____	_____

_____

E. COMPUTER TECHNOLOGY

14. Does your business information and reference service have CD-ROM databases? ____yes ____no

    If yes, which are available? (check as many as apply)
    ____ Compact Disclosure
    ____ ABI/INFORM
    ____ Business Abstracts
    ____ CIRR
    ____ Standard & Poor's Corporations
    ____ Thomas Register
    ____ other (please specify) _____
    _____
    _____

15. Which online vendor systems are available in your library? (check as many as apply)
    ____ BRS
    ____ Dow Jones News Retrieval
    ____ DIALOG
    ____ NewsNet
    ____ NEXIS
    ____ ORBIT
    ____ VU/TEXT
    ____ WILSONLINE
    ____ other (please specify) _____
    _____

16. Which of the following databases available online are most frequently searched for business/industry information? (check as many as apply)

    ____ ABI/INFORM
    ____ American Banker Full Text
    ____ BioBusiness
    ____ Business Dateline
    ____ Business Periodicals Index
    ____ Business Software Database
    ____ CENDATA
    ____ Chemical Industry Notes
    ____ D&B Donnelly Demographics
    ____ D&B Dun's Financial Records
    ____ Disclosure/Spectrum Ownership
    ____ Foods Adlibra
    ____ Health Planning and Administration
    ____ Investext
    ____ Labordoc
    ____ Management Contents
    ____ PAIS International
    ____ Pharmaceutical News Index
    ____ PTS Prompt
    ____ Standard & Poors News
    ____ Trade & Industry Index
    ____ Trademarkscan
    ____ other (please specify _____)

17. What limitations are placed on online searching? (check as many as apply)

    ____ a. charges
    ____ b. number of databases searched
    ____ c. number of citations printed
    ____ d. number of abstracts with citations printed
    ____ e. number of full text records printed
    ____ f. time spent on the search
    ____ g. other (please specify) _____

18. If your library charges for online searching, what is the policy? For example, connect time, printing charges, full cost, free up to $10.

19. Would limitations be waived for corporate personnel willing to pay full cost (including staff time) for in!depth research, monthly updates (SDI) on specific topic(s), for example? ____yes ____no

F. NETWORKS AND INTERLIBRARY LOAN

20. Does your library participate in any library networks?____yes
____no

If yes, please check as many as apply:
____ OCLC
____ RLIN
____ Michigan Library Consortium
____ WLN
____ UTLAS
____ other (please specify) _____

_____

_____

21. Please rate on a scale numbered from 1-5 the significance of the following to interlibrary loan use for supplementing the business collection. (least 1-2-3-4-5 most)
____ a. resources in other related subject fields
____ b. obscure or scholarly periodicals
____ c. dissertations/theses
____ d. back-file periodicals
____ e. government documents
____ f. company/industry data
____ g. other (please specify) _____

_____

22. Approximately what percent of your interlibrary loan requests are filled by corporate libraries? _____%

23. Approximately what percent of the interlibrary loan requests received by your library are from corporate libraries? _____%

G. BUDGET

24. Did your budget for business information and reference service increase, remain the same or decrease in the past fiscal year and in this fiscal year?

	increased same	remained the	decreased same
Past Fiscal	_____	_____	_____
This Fiscal	_____	_____	_____

25. Does your library receive benefits from corporations as a result of satisfaction with your service? ____yes ____no

If yes, what are the benefits? (check as many as apply)
   ____ a. funding/contributions
   ____ b. service subsidies
   ____ c. books/monographs
   ____ d. newspaper/journal subscriptions
   ____ e. equipment/computer systems
   ____ f. software
   ____ g. other (please specify) _____

   _____

   _____

26. Do contributions from corporations influence your decision to purchase business materials that have:
   ____ a. high potential use?
   ____ b. only occasional potential use?

H. EVALUATION

27. What data are collected to evaluate service to the business community? (check as many as apply)
   ____ a. percent of questions answered/not answered
   ____ b. analysis of the number of questions asked/answered/not answered
   ____ c. sources used to answer individual questions
   ____ d. number of CD-ROM/online database searches run and success rate/rate of accuracy
   ____ e. user satisfaction/interview or questionnaire results
   ____ f. results of study of use of networks/resource sharing
   ____ g. analysis of interlibrary loan requests/requests filled
   ____ h. number of referrals to special libraries/types of libraries used
   ____ i. assessment of collection development policy and procedure
   ____ j. other (please specify) _____

   _____

Thank you for completing the questionnaire.

Appendix B
Survey of Corporate Library Services

A. GENERAL INFORMATION

1. Is professional staff available: (check as many as apply)
    ___ a. evenings?
    ___ b. Saturdays?
    ___ c. Sundays?

B. COLLECTION

2. Which of the following best describes the organization of your library? (check one)
    ___ a. the main library in the corporation
    ___ b. main library with satellite libraries located in other corporate offices
    ___ c. a satellite library
    ___ d. other (please specify) _____
    _____

3. Does the collection include: (check as many as apply)
    ___ a. general reference titles (dictionaries, encyclopedias)
    ___ b. subject specific indexes
    ___ c. government documents
    ___ d. company reports/corporate data
    ___ e. company correspondence
    ___ f. association publications
    ___ g. specialized monographs

_____ h. data on domestic and foreign trends/activities

_____ i. market/consumer studies

_____ j. case histories pertaining to corporate activities and research

_____ k. industry data/statistics/trends

_____ l. general newspapers/journals

_____ m. subject and industry-specific newspapers/journals

_____ n. newspaper clipping file

_____ o. newsletters

_____ p. local/state regulations and reports

_____ q. doctoral dissertations and theses

_____ r. legal indexes/dictionaries/encyclopedias

_____ s. patent/trademark data

_____ t. fiction collection/paperback collection for casual reading

_____ u. non-fiction titles not specific to company needs

_____ v. other (please specify) _____

_____

If your library has a written collection policy, please send a copy.

C. SERVICES

4. Is your library open to the public? ____yes ____no

   If yes, what percentage are outside users? _____%

5. Which of the following services are available to corporate personnel/outside users? (check as many as apply)

Corporate Personnel	Outside Users	
_____	_____	a. ready-reference service (including photocopy)
_____	_____	b. retrieval of hard-to find or obscure information
_____	_____	c. mediated online database searching (librarian searches)
_____	_____	d. end-user searching of online databases (user searches)
_____	_____	e. end-user searching training programs
_____	_____	f. editing of downloaded search results prior to delivery in printed or electronic formats

Corporate Outside
Personnel Users

_____	_____	g. SDI service (Selective Dissemination of information)/monthly updates on specific topics, including bibliographic data and abstracts
_____	_____	h. interlibrary loan for items not in the collection
_____	_____	i. bibliographies of new items of interest to the corporation
_____	_____	j. telephone reference service
_____	_____	k. telefacsimile service
_____	_____	l. training programs on available resources and the use of the collection
_____	_____	m. other (please specify) _____

6. Are access or service limitations placed on outside users? (check as many as apply)

____ a. access available by appointment only
____ b. no access/service to high school students
____ c. access limited to graduate students and researchers
____ d. telephoned or written requests only
____ e. service limited to requests from other librarians
____ f. no online database searching
____ g. no end-user searching
____ h. service limited to only interlibrary loan requests and photocopies
____ i. no access to company records/research studies
____ j. fees charged (please specify) _____

____ k. other (please specify) _____

7. Does your library actively market service to
____corporate personnel ____outside users?

If yes, is it promoted by such media as: (check as many as apply)

Corporate Outside
Personnel Users

_____	_____	a. library newsletter
_____	_____	b. newspaper ads/articles
_____	_____	c. radio/television

Corporate   Outside
Personnel   Users
_____	_____	d. bookmarks/flyers/posters
_____	_____	e. exhibits at business/industry fairs and conventions
_____	_____	f. subject bibliographies
_____	_____	g. lists of new acquisitions
_____	_____	h. bibliographies with abstracts on new data/research
_____	_____	i. direct mail campaigns
_____	_____	j. special fee-based research service for outside users
_____	_____	k. visits to public libraries
_____	_____	l. other (please specify)
_____	_____	_____
_____	_____	_____

D. COOPERATION AND PUBLIC LIBRARIES

8. Which libraries do you cooperate with? (check as many as apply)
   _____ a. public libraries
   _____ b. college/university libraries
   _____ c. association libraries
   _____ d. other corporate libraries
   _____ e. other (please specify) _____

9. If your library does not cooperate with public libraries, please explain:

10. Are corporation personnel made aware of the resources and services available in public libraries? _____yes _____no

11. Do you refer corporate personnel to public libraries?
    _____yes _____no
    If yes, do you give: (check as many as apply)
    _____ a. name, location and library hours given?
    _____ b. corporate librarian calls public library to arrange for patron visit?
    _____ c. corporate librarian calls public librarian to explain the request?
    _____ d. corporate librarian obtains information from public library and delivers it to patron?
    _____ e. other (please specify) _____

12. Please rate on a scale numbered from 1-5 the resources which are most frequently requested from public libraries? (least 1-2-3-4-5 most)

    ____ books/monographs related to individual requests not available in your library

    ____ articles from journals not available in your library data on particular corporation

    ____ information on research findings in a particular industry/corporation

    ____ medical/legal/technical research data

    ____ special indexes/bibliographies/dictionaries

    ____ government documents/reports

    ____ online databases not available in your library or not searched

    ____ CD-ROM databases not available in your library

    ____ other (please specify) _____

13. Do public libraries impose service limitations on the patrons you refer to them? ____yes ____no

If yes, please explain: _____

_____

_____

14. Has cooperation with public libraries increased:

    a. in the past fiscal year? ____yes ____no

    b. in this fiscal year? ____yes ____no

If yes, what are the reasons? (check as many as apply)

	Past Fiscal	This Fiscal
inadequate budget/rising cost of materials	_____	_____
need for reference resources not available in the library	_____	_____
public library has developed a business information service that fills needs rapidly and thoroughly	_____	_____
greater demand for a variety of journals located using online databases	_____	_____
membership in cooperative networks and the expected resource sharing/reciprocation	_____	_____
corporate library listings in library directories	_____	_____
other (please specify)		
_____	_____	_____
_____	_____	_____

E. COMPUTER TECHNOLOGY

15. Does your library have CD-ROM databases? ____yes ____no

    If yes, which are available? (check as many as apply)
    ____ Compact Disclosure
    ____ ABI/INFORM
    ____ Abstracts
    ____ CIRR
    ____ Standard & Poor's Corporations
    ____ Thomas Register
    ____ other (please specify) _____
    _____

16. Which online vendor systems are available in your library? (check as many as apply)
    ____ BRS
    ____ Dow Jones News Retrieval
    ____ DIALOG
    ____ NewsNet
    ____ NEXIS
    ____ ORBIT
    ____ VU/TEXT
    ____ WILSONLINE
    ____ other (please specify) _____
    _____

17. Are these systems used to search only databases that are specific to the corporation's needs? ____yes ____no

    If databases are searched for other than corporate-specific information, is the employee charged a fee? ____yes ____no

18. Is online database searching available to outside users? ____yes ____no

19. Which of the databases available online are most frequently requested by corporate personnel/outside users? (check as many as apply)

Corporate Personnel	Outside Users	
_____	_____	ABI/INFORM
_____	_____	American Banker Full Text
_____	_____	BioBusiness
_____	_____	Business Dateline
_____	_____	Business Periodicals Index

Corporate Personnel	Outside Users	
_____	_____	Business Software Database
_____	_____	CENDATA
_____	_____	Chemical Industry Notes
_____	_____	D&B Donnelly Demographics
_____	_____	D&B Dun's Financial Records
_____	_____	Disclosure/Spectrum Ownership
_____	_____	Foods Adlibra
_____	_____	Health Planning and Administration
_____	_____	Investext
_____	_____	Labordoc
_____	_____	Management Contents
_____	_____	PAIS International
_____	_____	Pharmaceutical News Index
_____	_____	PTS Prompt
_____	_____	Standard & Poors News
_____	_____	Trade & Industry Index
_____	_____	Trademarkscan
		other (please specify)
_____	_____	_____
_____	_____	_____

20. What limitations are placed on online searching for corporate personnel/outside users? (check as many as apply)

Corporate Personnel	Outside Users	
_____	_____	a. charges
_____	_____	b. number of databases searched
_____	_____	c. number of citations printed
_____	_____	d. number of abstracts with citations printed
_____	_____	e. number of full text records printed
_____	_____	f. time spent on the search
		g. other (please specify)
_____	_____	_____
_____	_____	_____

21. If your library charges for online searching, what is the policy for corporate personnel/outside users?

22. Would limitations be waived for outside users willing to pay full cost, including staff time? ____yes ____no

F. NETWORKS AND INTERLIBRARY LOAN

23. Does your library participate in any library networks? ____yes
____no

If yes, please check as many as apply:
____ OCLC
____ RLIN
____ Michigan Library Consortium
____ WLN
____ UTLAS
____ other (please specify) _____
_____
_____

24. Please rate on a scale numbered from 1-5 the significance of the following to interlibrary loan use for supplementing the collection. (least 1-2-3-4-5 most)
____ a. resources in other subject fields
____ b. obscure/scholarly periodicals
____ c. dissertations/theses
____ d. back-file periodicals
____ e. general newspapers/journals
____ f. government documents
____ g. other corporate/industry data
____ h. other (please specify) _____
_____

25. Which materials are most frequently obtained from public libraries?

Approximately what percent of your interlibrary loan requests are filled by public libraries? _____%

26. Which materials are most frequently requested by public libraries?

Approximately what percent of your interlibrary loan requests are from public libraries? _____%

G. BUDGET

27. Did your budget increase, remain the same or decrease in the past year and in this fiscal year?

	increased same	remained the	decreased
Past Fiscal	_____	_____	_____
This Fiscal	_____	_____	_____

28. Does your corporation compensate public libraries as a result of satisfaction with their services? ____yes ____no

    If yes, how are they compensated? (check as many as apply)
    _____ a. funding/contributions
    _____ b. service subsidies
    _____ c. books/monographs
    _____ d. newspaper/journal subscriptions
    _____ e. equipment/computer systems
    _____ f. software
    _____ g. other (please specify) _____
    _____

29. Does the availability of certain resources and services in the public library influence your decision not to acquire them for your library? ____yes ____no

H. EVALUATION

30. What data are collected to evaluate library service? (check as many as apply)
    _____ a. percent of questions answered/not answered
    _____ b. analysis of the number of questions asked/answered/not answered
    _____ c. sources used to answer individual questions
    _____ d. number of CD-ROM/online database searches run and success rate/rate of accuracy
    _____ e. user satisfaction/interview or questionnaire results
    _____ f. results of study of use of networks/resource sharing
    _____ g. analysis of interlibrary loan requests/requests filled
    _____ h. count of number of referrals to other libraries/types of libraries used
    _____ i. assessment of collection development policy and procedure
    _____ j. other (please specify) _____
    _____
    _____

Thank you for completing the questionnaire.

Appendix C
Survey of Academic Library Service to the Business Community

1. Do you serve the business community: (check all that apply)
   ____locally?   ____within your state?   ____out of state?

2. Please rate on a scale numbered from 1-5 the frequency of use of your service by the following user groups: (least 1-2-3-4-5 most)
   ____ a. corporate personnel
   ____ b. personnel of small/medium size businesses
   ____ c. entrepreneurs/self-employed
   ____ d. researchers/technicians
   ____ e. government officials
   ____ f. corporate library staff
   ____ g. public library staff
   ____ h. job seekers
   ____ i. students from other colleges/universities
   ____ j. other (please specify) _____

3. Please describe briefly the services/collection available to the business community:
   _____
   _____
   _____
   _____
   _____

4 . Are access or service limitations imposed on members of the business community? (For example, by appointment only, affiliation with corporation, no online searching, no manual searching, no book loans.)

_____

_____

_____

_____

_____

5. Please rate on a scale numbered from 1-5 the resources which are most frequently requested by members of the business community: (least 1-2-3-4-5 most)
   _____ a. books/monographs
   _____ b. journal articles
   _____ c. corporate data
   _____ d. research findings for a particular industry/corporation
   _____ e. medical/legal/technical research data
   _____ f. government documents/reports
   _____ g. online databases
   _____ h. other (please specify) _____

   _____

   _____

6. Has your service to the business community increased in:
   _____ a. the past fiscal year?   _____ b. this fiscal year?

   If yes, what are the reasons? (please explain)

   _____

   _____

7. Which online services are available? (check as many as apply)
   _____ a. BRS   _____ b. Dow Jones News Retrieval
   _____ c. DIALOG   _____ d. NewsNet
   _____ e. LEXIS/NEXIS_____ f. ORBIT
   _____ g. VU/TEXT   _____ h. WILSONLINE
   _____ i. other (please specify) _____

   _____

   _____

8. Which databases available online are most frequently searched for members of the business community? (please list)

   _____

   _____

   _____

9. What are the charges for:
   a. online searching? _____
   b. manual searching? _____
   c. photocopies? _____
   d. FAX service? _____
   e. book loans? _____
   f. translation service? _____
   g. faculty consultation? _____
   h. other (please specify) _____
   _____

10. What is your request acceptance/payment policy for services available to members of the business community? (please explain)
    _____
    _____
    _____
    _____
    _____

11. Is your service actively marketed to the business community?
    ____yes ____no

    If yes, how is it promoted? (please explain)
    _____
    _____
    _____
    _____
    _____

12. Do you evaluate your service to the business community? ____yes ____no

    If yes, what data are collected? (please explain)
    _____
    _____
    _____
    _____
    _____

Thank you for completing the questionnaire.

Bibliography

"Access Colorado." *Public Libraries* 32 (January/February 1993): 48.

Andros, Peter. "Bullish on the Bookmobile: The Story of Public Library Service to Dow Jones & Company, Inc." *Wilson Library Bulletin* 67 (May 1993): 50-1.

"Anne Arundel Public Library To Charge Fees: Maryland Library to Charge for Out-of-System ILLs; Economy Blamed." *Library Journal* 118 (April 15, 1993): 23.

"Arizona State Folds Fee-Based Service." *Library Journal* 118 (April 1, 1993): 24-9.

Baker, Sharon L. "Improving Business Services Through the Use of Focus Groups." *RQ* 30 (Spring 1991): 377-85.

Ball, Dannie J. "Current Issues in Reference and Adult Services." *RQ* 27 (Winter 1987): 171-74.

Barnett, Philip. "Closing the Corporate Library: Some Personal Reflections." *Special Libraries* 83 (Fall 1992): 237-41.

Barry, Maria C. "Quality: An Essential Ingredient." *Specialist* 15 (February 1992): 1+.

Basch, Reva. "Local Motion: Regional Databases for Business Information." *Database* 15 (June 1992): 22-7.

Bender, David R. "False Savings: A Reminder for Corporate Leaders." *Specialist* (January 1992): 8.

Bentley, Stella, and Cheryl LaGuardia. "Black Holes in the Library Universe: Budgeting for Computerized Information." *Proceedings of the Fourteenth National Online Meeting—1993*. Medford, NJ: Learned Information, 1993.

Berry, John. "CD-ROM: The Medium and the Moment." *Library Journal* 117 (February 1, 1992): 45!7.

Bjorner, Susan N. "Patent and Trademark Databases: Intellectual Property for the Masses." *Link-Up* 9 (July/August 1992): 14-15+.

Bluh, Pamela. "Document Delivery 2000: Will it Change the Nature of Librarianship." *Wilson Library Bulletin* 67 (February 1993): 49-51+.

Bolt, Nancy. "Libraries, Public Policy, and Economic Development." *Library Administration & Management* 3 (Spring 1991): 81-5.

Boylan, Lee. "Going Over the Wall." *Unabashed Librarian* 54 (1985): 5-6.

Brimsek, Tobi A., comp. *From the Top: Profiles of U.S. and Canadian Corporate Libraries and Information Centers.* Washington, DC: Special Libraries Association, 1989.

Brody, Roberta. "End-Users in 1993: After a Decade." *Online* 17 (May 1993): 66-9.

Buckland, Michael. *Redesigning Library Services: A Manifesto.* Chicago: American Library Association, 1992.

Burgess, Dean. "Fee or Free: The Data Base Access Controversy." *Reference Librarian* 12 (Spring/Summer 1985): 105-15.

Canning, Joan. "Serving Business in a Changing Business Climate." *Bookmark* 47 (Fall 1988): 17-19.

Caren, Loretta, and Arleen Somerville. "Issues Facing Private Academic Libraries Considering Fee-Based Programs." In *Information Brokers and Reference Service,* edited by Robin Kinder and Bill Katz. New York: Haworth Press, 1988: 37-49.

Coffman, Steve, ed. *FISCAL Directory of Fee-Based Information Services in Libraries.* Los Angeles: County of Los Angeles Public Library, 1990.

_____, and Pat Wiedensohler, comps. *FISCAL Directory of Fee-Based Research and Document Supply Services.* Chicago: American Library Association, 1993.

Colson, John Calvin. "Form Against Function: The American Public Library and Contemporary Society." *Journal of Library History* 18 (Spring 1983): 111-42.

Coon, Carol. "San Francisco Public Library Small Business Resources." *Unabashed Librarian* 56 (1985): 21.

Criswell, Sharon, and Bill Howie. "A Resource Center Without Walls: SMU's Business Information Center." *Library Journal* 114 (June 1, 1989): 69-73.

DeWitt, Karen. "The Nation's Library for a Fee and a Modem." *New York Times* Sec. 4 (February 28, 1993): 16.

Dillman, Don. "Community Needs and the Rural Public Library." *Wilson Library Bulletin* 65 (May 1991): 31-3+.

DiMattia, Susan S. "Corporations and Library Fundraising." *Library Journal* 109 (February 1, 1984): 139-44.

_____. "Taking Care of Business." *Library Journal* 117 (March 15, 1992): 42-8.

DuRoy, Sheryl. "Patents as Business Information Sources." *Public Library Quarterly* 6 (Summer 1985): 3-14.

Dustin, M.J. "The MINITEX Reference Service: A Publicly Funded Information Broker." In *Information Brokers and Reference Services,* edited by Robin Kinder and Bill Katz. New York: Haworth Press, 1988: 133-43.

"Economic Regeneration: Does the Public Library Have a Role?" *Public Library Journal* 5 (May/June 1990): 57-9.

"Entrepreneurship." *Unabashed Librarian* 70 (1989): 15-16.

Ernest, Douglas J. "Academic Libraries, Fee-Based Information Services, and the Business Community." *RQ* 32 (Spring 1993): 393-402.

Everett, David. "Full-Text Online Databases and Document Delivery in an Academic Library: Too Little Too Late." *Online* 17 (March 1993): 22-25.

Favini, Robert. "Job Hunter's Search for Company Information: Success with

Last-Minute Requests Using Standard Business Sources." *RQ* 31 (Winter 1991): 155-61.

Ferguson, Elizabeth and Emily R. Mobley. *Special Libraries at Work*. Hamden, CT: Library Professional Publications, 1984.

Ganly, John. "There and Nowhere Else." *Bookmark* 47 (Fall 1988): 15-16.

Garnett, Emily. "Reference Service by Telephone." *Library Journal* 61 (December 1, 1936): 909-11.

George, Lee Anne. "Fee-Based Information Services and Document Delivery." *Wilson Library Bulletin* 67 (February 1993): 41-44 +.

Gilton, Donna L. "Information Entrepreneurship: Sources for Reference Librarians." *RQ* 31 (Spring 1992): 346-55.

Goldberg, Susan. "Community Action Now: Defying the Doomsayers." *Library Journal* 118 (March 15, 1993): 29-32.

Grodin, Erica. "We're Good for Business." *Bookmark* 47 (Fall 1988): 43-4.

Grosch, Mary Frances. "Business Reference Sources for the Public Library." *Illinois Libraries* 70 (November 1988): 607-12.

Hane, Paula. "Access to Government Information." *Database* 15 (October 1992): 8-9.

_____. "Database Delicacies on the Internet." *Database* 16 (June 1993): 6!7.

Hanson, Carl A., ed. *Librarian at Large: Selected Writings of John Cotton Dana*. Washington, DC: Special Libraries Association, 1991.

Harper, Patricia. "Libraries and Business: Can They Form a Better Partnership." *Illinois Libraries* 68 (September 1986): 417-18.

Hattendorf, Lynn C. "Art of Reference Collection Development." *RQ* 29 (Winter 1989): 219-29.

Hawbaker, A. Craig, and Judith M. Nixon. *Industry and Company Information: Illustrated Search Strategy and Sources*. Ann Arbor, MI: Pierian Press, 1991.

Hernon, Peter. "Utility Measures, Not Performance Measures for Library Reference Service?" *RQ* 26 (Summer 1987): 449-59.

Hill, Linda. "Issues in Network Participation for Corporate Librarians." *Special Libraries* 76 (Winter 1985): 2-10.

Hlava, Marjorie M. K. "The Internationalization of the Information Industry." In *Bulletin of the American Society for Information Science* 19 (February/March 1993): 12-15.

Houlahan, John. "Looking at Rural Libraries Through Rose-Colored Glasses." *Wilson Library Bulletin* 65 (May 1991): 36-8.

Ison, Jan. "Dynamics of Future Cooperation." *Wilson Library Bulletin* 65 (May 1991): 41-5.

Jackson, Mary E. "Document Delivery Over the Internet." *Online* 17 (March 1993): 14-21.

Jehlik, Theresa. "Putting Knowledge to Work." *Public Library Quarterly* 9 (1989): 13-30.

Kenney, Donald J., and Gail McMillan. "State Library Associations: How Well Do They Support Professional Development?" *RQ* 31 (Spring 1992): 377-84.

Kountz, John. "Tomorrow's Libraries: More Than a Modular Telephone Jack, Less Than a Complete Revolution." *Library Hi Tech* 40 10:4 (1992): 39-50.

Kruzas, Anthony Thomas. *Business and Industrial Libraries in the United States, 1820-1940.* New York: Special Libraries Association, 1965.

"LA County Public Library Opens Fee-Based Service." *Wilson Library Bulletin* 64 (September 1989): 18-19.

"LA County Starts Fee-Based Service for Businesses." *Library Journal* 114 (September 1, 1989): 134.

Lachman, Christine E. "Fax-On-Demand: An Introduction." *Library Hi Tech* 9 (1991): 7-24.

Ladner, Sharyn J. "Resource Sharing in Sci-Tech and Business Libraries: Formal Networking Practices." *Special Libraries* 83 (Spring 1992): 96-112.

LaQuey, Tracy, and Jeanne C. Ryer. *The Internet Companion.* New York: Addison Wesley, 1992.

LaRue, James. "A Superhighway to the World: The Birth of the Access Colorado Library and Information Network." *Wilson Library Bulletin* 67 (May 1993): 35-7.

Leggett, Mark, and Betty Tomeo. "Fueling the Entrepreneurial Dream: Small Business Resources." *RQ* 29 (Spring 1990): 341-7.

Libraries, Users and Copyright: Proprietary Rights and Wrongs. Joseph Shubert and E.J. Josey, editors of The Bookmark. Vol. 50, no.2, Winter 1992.

"Library Buys Piece of Altman's." *New York Times* Sec. 10 (February 28, 1993): 1.

"Library Without Walls." *Information Today* 9 (February 1992): 7.

Linden, Margaret J. "Networking Among Chevron Libraries." *Special Libraries* 80 (Spring 1989): 125-9.

Major, Jean A. "Library Service for Small Business: An Exploratory Study." *RQ* 30 (Fall 1990): 27-31.

Malecki, Paul A. "Following in Ben Franklin's Footsteps: Public Library Business Services in Rural Areas." *Bookmark* 47 (Fall 1988): 50-55.

Malinconico, S. Michael. "Information's Brave New World." *Library Journal* 117 (May 1, 1992): 36!40.

Manley, Marian C., and Beatrice Winser. *Business Service in Public Libraries of 109 Large Cities.* Newark, NJ: Newark New Jersey Free Public Library, Business Branch, 1930.

Marvin, Stephen. "ExeLS: Executive Library Services." In *Information Brokers and Reference Services,* edited by Robin Kinder and Bill Katz. New York: HaworthPress, 1988: 145-60.

Masten, John. "Education, Libraries, and the National Information Infrastructure." *Library Hi Tech News* 102 (May 1993): 1-3.

Matarazzo, James M. *Corporate Library Excellence.* Washington, DC: Special Libraries Association, 1990.

Matarazzo, James M. and Laurence Prusak. *Valuing Corporate Libraries.* Washington, DC: Special Libraries Association, 1990.

_____. "Valuing Corporate Libraries: A Senior Management Survey." *Special Libraries* 81 (Spring 1990): 102-10.

Moody, Marilyn. "Government Information." *RQ* 27 (Spring 1988): 322-32.

"Multnomah May Charge for Telephone Reference." *American Libraries* 24 (April 1993): 288-90.

"Multnomah To Charge for Phone Reference." *Library Journal* 118 (April 1, 1993): 20-24.

Nevins, Allan, and Henry Steele Commager. *Pocket History of the United States.* 9th ed. New York: Pocket Books, 1992.

"NYNEX Announces Fast Track Business Disc." *Information Today* 9 (July/August 1992): 15.

"NYPL's Science Library Gets $9.5 M." *Library Journal* 118 (May 15, 1993):18.

Ojala, Marydee. "A Model for Quality Business Searching." *Online* 17 (March 1993): 77-79.

_____. "Decision Points for Company Research." *Online* 17 (January 1993): 79-82.

_____. "Past Facts: Business History Searching." *Database* 16 (February 1993): 88-90.

_____. "Public Library Business Collections and New Reference Technologies." *Special Libraries* 74 (April 1983): 138-49.

_____. "Statistical and Numeric Databases for Business." *Database* 16 (June 1993): 99-101.

O'Leary, Mick. "New Roles for Information Searchers." *Online* 17 (May 1993): 10-11.

_____. "Quint Advises Amateur Searchers." *Link-Up* 10 (MaypJune 1993): 15+.

Paster, Amy, and Bonnie Osif. "Great Expectations: Satisfying Today's Patrons." *Special Libraries* 83 (Fall 1992): 195-98.

Penniman, W. David. "The Library of Tomorrow: A Universal Window Serving Independent Problem Solvers." *Library Hi Tech* 40 10:4 (1992): 23-26.

Phenix, Katharine. "LITA Meets in Denver: Opening Tollgates to the Electronic Highway." *Wilson Library Bulletin* 67 (December 1992): 58-60.

Quint, Barbara. "The Big Lie." *Information Today* 10 (April 1993): 7-9.

_____. "The Dead Database: Where Do Databases Go When They Leave Online?" *Database* 5 (October 1992): 15-31.

_____. "Win or Lose." *Wilson Library Bulletin* 67 (February 1993): 72-4.

Riechel, Rosemarie. *Improving Telephone Information and Reference Service in Public Libraries.* Hamden, CT: Library Professional Publications, 1987.

Rose, Robert F. "Conducting Research on Potential Employers: Report on a Cooperative Workshop." *RQ* 27 (Spring 1988): 404-9.

Rosen, Brenda C. "The Age of the Information Broker: An Introduction." In *Information Brokers and Reference Services,* edited by Robin Kinder and Bill Katz. New York: Haworth Press, 1988: 5-16.

Rosen, Linda. "The Information Professional as Knowledge Engineer." Parts I,2. *Information Today* 10 (April, May 1993): 57-60, 47-9.

Rush, James E. "In the Name of Access: The Economics of Information Dissemination." *Bulletin of the American Society for Information Science* 19 (December/January 1993): 13-15.

Schlessinger, Bernard S. *The Basic Business Library: Core Resources.* 2nd ed. Phoenix, AZ: Oryx Press, 1989.

"Service to Small Business Lauded in Bay Co. Michigan." *Library Journal* 111 (July 1986): 21.

Seymour, Whitney North, comp. *The Changing Role of Public Libraries.* Metuchen, NJ: Scarecrow Press, 1980.

_____, and Elizabeth N. Layne. *For the People-Fighting for Public Libraries.* Garden City, NY: Doubleday, 1979.

Shirley, Beverley. "State Library Survey Online Search Services." *Special Libraries* 84 (Spring 1993): 95-103.

Small Business, Big Challenge: Providing Information to Small Business and the Entrepreneur. RASD Occasiona Papers, No.15. Chicago: Reference and Adult Services Division, American Library Association, 1992.

Smith, Barbara. "A Strategic Approach to Online User Fees in Public Libraries." *Library Journal* 114 (February 1, 1989): 33-6.

Smith, Wendy. "Fee-Based Services: Are They Worth It?" *Library Journal* 118 (June 15, 1993):40-3.

Smith-Burnett, Leticia. "A Public Information Service to the Offshore Service Industry: The Commercial and Technical Department of Aberdeen City Libraries." *SLA News* 192 (March/April 1986): 20-23.

Stankus, Tony. "Alert Collector." *RQ* 29 (Spring 1990: 341-6.

"Statewide Reference Center in Missouri." *Wilson Library Bulletin* 67 (December 1992): 12.

Steckel, Richard. "Doing Good in Challenging Times." *Wilson Library Bulletin* 67 (December 1992): 43-5.

Steele, Jane. "Economic Regeneration: Does the Public Library Have a Role?" *Public Library Journal* 5 (May/June 1990): 57-9.

Stein, Carolyn. "Speaking the Language of Business: The Denver Public Library Serves Business Needs, But Not All Its Own Needs Are Being Met." *Colorado Business Magazine* 17 (February 1990): 48-50.

Stieg, Margaret F. "Fee vs Free in Historical Perspective." *Reference Librarian* 12 (Spring/Summer 1985): 93-103.

Stranathan, Helen E. and Ralph W. Teller. "Computers and Interlibrary Loan: A Boon to the Rural Community." *Colorado Libraries* 14 (June 1988): 15-16.

Sweeney, Dell, and Karin Zilla, eds. *Position Descriptions in Special Libraries.* 2nd ed. Washington, DC: Special Libraries Association, 1992.

Sweetland, James H. "Information Poverty—Let Me Count the Ways." *Database* 16 (August 1993): 8-10.

Tenopir, Carol. "Full Text on CD-ROM." *Library Journal* 117 (July 1992): 50-51.

The Information Society: Issues and Answers. New York: Neal-Schuman, 1978.

Trott, Fiona. "Information for Small Firms—The Relevance of Public Information Service." *Library Association Record* 87 (July 1985): 259.

_____. and John Martyn. "An Information Service for Small Firms from a Public Library Base." *ASLIB Proceedings* 38 (February 1986): 43-50.

"$23 Million in Bonds Issued for NYPL." *Library Journal* 117 (September 15, 1992): 14.

"U.S. Labor and Employment Laws on HRIN." *Information Today* 9 (July/August 1992): 4.

Valauskas, Edward J. "Copyright: Know Your Electronic Rights!" *Library Journal* 117 (August 1992): 41-3.

Voight, Kathleen J. "Computer Search Services and Information Brokering in Academic Libraries." In *Information Brokers and Reference Services*, edited by Robin Kinder and Bill Katz. New York: Haworth Press, 1988: 17-36.

"Vu/Text Papers to be Transfered by End of Year." *Link-Up* 9 (September/October 1992): 11.

Warner, Alice Sizer. *Making Money: Fees for Library Services*. New York: Neal-Schuman, 1989.

Watson, Bob. "Reference Services in an Information Age: A Public Library Perspective." *RQ* 31 (Summer 1992): 499-506.

_____, and Lawrence Boyle. "Growth of a Business Directory." *RQ* 31 (Fall 1992): 10-13.

Watts, E. Spencer, and Alan R. Samuels. "What Business Are We In? Perceptions of the Roles and Purposes of the Pyblic Library as Reflected in Professional Literature." *Public Libraries* 23 (Winter 1984): 130-4.

Webb, Joseph A. "DataTimes They Are A-Changin'." *Link-Up* 9 (March/April 1992): 14-15+.

White, Herbert S. "Putting Users to Work." *Library Journal* 113 (March 15, 1988): 40-41.

White, Lawrence J. *The Public Library in the 1980s*. Lexington, MA: D.C. Heath, 1983.

Williams, Martha. "Highlights of the Online/CD-ROM Database Industry." *Proceedings of the Fourteenth National Online Meeting—1993*. Medford, NJ: Learned Information, 1993.

"Wilson Business Abstracts on CD-ROM." *Information Today* 9 (July/August 1992): 21-2.

Wressell, Pat. "Marketing Advice: A New Role for Libraries?" *Library Association Record* 92 (March 1990): 189-91+.

"Year 2000: Dreams and Nightmares." *Searcher* 1 (May, June 1993): 16-18, 26-29.

Zilm, Gwen. "Meeting the Needs of Canada's Small Businesses." *Canadian Library Journal* 45 (April 1988): 109-12.

Index

6206 080

Réseau de...
Universiré d...
Échéance